BFI FILM CLASSICS

∙∙∙∙∙∙∙∙∙∙∙∙∙∙∙∙∙∙∙∙∙∙∙∙

Edward Buscombe
SERIES EDITOR

Cinema is a fragile medium. Many of the great classic films of the past now exist, if at all, in damaged or incomplete prints. Concerned about the deterioration in the physical state of our film heritage, the National Film and Television Archive, a Division of the British Film Institute, has compiled a list of 360 key films in the history of the cinema. The long-term goal of the Archive is to build a collection of perfect show-prints of these films, which will then be screened regularly at the Museum of the Moving Image in London in a year-round repertory.

BFI Publishing has now commissioned a series of books to stand alongside these titles. Authors, including film critics and scholars, film-makers, novelists, historians and those distinguished in the arts, have been invited to write on a film of their choice, drawn from the Archive's list. Each volume will present the author's own insights into the chosen film, together with a brief production history and a detailed filmography, notes and bibliography. The numerous illustrations have been specially made from the Archive's own prints.

With new titles published each year, the BFI Film Classics series is rapidly growing into an authoritative and highly readable guide to the great films of world cinema.

D1595465

Gloria Grahame and Nicholas Ray with the script of *In a Lonely Place*

BFI FILM

CLASSICS

IN A LONELY PLACE

....

Dana Polan

BRITISH FILM INSTITUTE

bfi

BFI PUBLISHING

LIBRARY
COLBY-SAWYER COLLEGE
NEW LONDON, NH 03257

PN
1997
.I4733
P65
1993
c.1

First published in 1993 by the
BRITISH FILM INSTITUTE
21 Stephen Street, London W1P 1PL

#29597491
Copyright © Dana Polan 1993

The British Film Institute exists
to encourage the development of film, television
and video in the United Kingdom,
and to promote knowledge, understanding and
enjoyment of the culture of the moving image.
Its activities include the National Film and
Television Archive; the National Film Theatre;
the Museum of the Moving Image;
the London Film Festival; the production and
distribution of film and video; funding and support for
regional activities; Library and Information Services;
Stills, Posters and Design; Research,
Publishing and Education; and the monthly
Sight and Sound magazine.

British Library Cataloguing in Publication Data

Polan, Dana
  In a Lonely Place – (Film Classics Series)
  I. Title   II. Series
  791.43

ISBN 0–85170–360–7

Designed by
Andrew Barron & Collis Clements Associates

Typesetting by
Fakenham Photosetting Limited, Norfolk

Printed in Great Britain by
The Trinity Press, Worcester

CONTENTS

For Agathe and Clémentine,
'futures cinéphiles'

ACKNOWLEDGMENTS

I wish to offer my deepest thanks to a number of friends and associates who aided in the research on *In a Lonely Place*: Bernard Eisenschitz, Nicholas Ray scholar *par excellence*, who offered good thoughts and graciously shared with me his own research materials (and whose massive biography of Ray is essential for anyone working on the director); Jessica Ullery, my research assistant for Fall 1992, who did a marvellous job at tracking down materials with great initiative and enthusiasm (especially for Bogart's 'Panda' incident); University of Pittsburgh graduate student Elayne Tobin, who used part of an internship at the British Film Institute to comb its wonderful library for materials on the film and on Nicholas Ray; Jan Young and Jeff Protzman, for tape lends and all-around good film conversation; my colleague James Knapp for insightful thoughts on J.M. Synge; Robert Sklar, who shared with me perceptions from his research on Humphrey Bogart; Doug Rathgeb, budding librarian, who took time from his own work on Nicholas Ray's *Rebel Without a Cause* to build bibliographies for me; Mrs Colette North, who offered reminiscences of her husband, Edmund North, credited with the adaptation of the film from Dorothy B. Hughes's novel; Dorothy B. Hughes, who shared reminiscences about negotiations for Hollywood adaptations of her books; David Bordwell, Thomas Elsaesser, and Tara Cuddihy (of *Ellery Queen Mystery Magazine*), who sent me copies of hard-to-track-down essays; Ed Buscombe, who was a marvellous and patient editor.

Many of these persons read and offered feedback on a draft of this study, as did colleagues in the wonderful programme in Film Studies at the University of Pittsburgh: John Groch (who also cued me in to the Smithereens), Marcia Landy, Lucy Fischer.

I also had the benefit of good collections and helpful staffs at the Film Section of the Museum of Modern Art, New York; the Theatre and Film Collection at Lincoln Center; the library of FEMIS, Paris (formerly IDHEC); the Médiathèque of Montélimar; the libraries of the University of Southern California and the Los Angeles Public Library. Markku Salmi of the BFI checked the credits.

My deepest appreciation goes to Donie Durieu for support – moral, intellectual, emotional.

The opening shot behind the credits

'IN A LONELY PLACE'

. . . .

Lots of stories get told in *In a Lonely Place*. Some of these help to move the plot along, such as the various stories that people tell Laurel Gray (Gloria Grahame) of past violence on the part of her love, Dix Steele (Humphrey Bogart). Some of the stories serve characters as tools to manipulate other people, as we see when Dix tells his agent that his (Dix's) interrogation by the police was a question of one story against another but that he, a screenwriter, told his story better. But intriguingly several of the stories that characters tell work to compare the film of *In a Lonely Place* itself to typical Hollywood fictions, and thereby to signal that the film is something other than just a standard formula.

Take for instance the plot of the big, fat romance novel *Althea Bruce* that Dix Steele is supposed to adapt as a film. From the start, it is obvious that Dix Steele doesn't even want to read a novel he assumes is trashy, and as hat-check girl Mildred Atkinson begins to tell the story of the novel to him it seems clear that the film shares his opinion. *Althea Bruce* is one sort of fiction; *In a Lonely Place* is something quite different. Indeed, as Mildred tells of the very rich Althea's attempt to make Channing the lifeguard jealous by seducing her lawyer in front of an open window which Channing can see into, Dix himself will go to his window and see Laurel Gray looking down at him from her balcony and in the exchange of glances a budding romance will intensify. Against the supposed florid mush of *Althea Bruce* ('She wants him terribly – his arms around her,' quotes Mildred), *In a Lonely Place* promotes itself as an uncompromising, unexaggerated look at love in a real world.

Or take the famous scene in which Laurel and Dix talk together in the kitchen. Laurel's suspicions of Dix's violent tendencies have already begun, as has Dix's desire to hold on to Laurel at all costs. In a long shot that emphasises their separation, Dix and Laurel take up positions on opposite sides of the room; the few close-ups in the scene cut each off from the other and emphasise their differing investments in a relationship gone out of sync. Even as Laurel knows her love is falling apart, she tells Dix how much she liked the love scene in his script. Dix replies, 'That's because they're not always telling each other how much in love they are. A good love scene should be about something besides love. For instance, this one: me fixing grapefruit, you sitting over there, dopey, half asleep. Anyone looking at us could tell we were in love.' Here, again, the film invites a comparison of Hollywood fiction and its own vision of love; it calls out emphatically to us to make the contrast since we are an audience watching as Dix talks of an audience watching. And there's a nice ambiguity in the past tense in Dix's last phrase ('we *were* in love'), for what the scene captures is the ways in which Dix and Laurel's romance is quickly becoming a thing of the past: when Dix follows this speech with a proposal of marriage, a close-up on Laurel confirms that whatever love she had has increasingly fallen into doubt.[1]

In such moments, *In a Lonely Place* marks its difference from typical Hollywood plots and gropes toward another identity. But what sort of film is *In a Lonely Place?* There's a strangeness to it. A film about the break-up of the old Hollywood, it echoes that break-up in its own style (for example, a curious blend of claustrophobic scenes filmed on studio sets and harsh on-location scenes typical of postwar open-air filming); a film about the break-up of romance in the postwar moment, it replays the offscreen romantic problems of its Hollywood film-makers and, more broadly, taps into postwar tensions in the American mythology of perfect love. Not for nothing does the vaguely punkish pop band, the Smithereens, condense dialogue from the film into a model song of lost love, 'In a Lonely Place' (from their album, *Especially for You*, 1986): 'I'm in a lonely place without you ... I was born the day I met you, lived a while when you loved me, died a little when we broke apart. Yesterday, it would have mattered; now today it doesn't mean a thing.'

As we trace *In a Lonely Place* from original idea to critical commentary, we find a production that quests for ways to define itself, that sets out to define the nature of romance and violence and of the two together, and that offers no one view but rather a series of possible images, possible identities.

. . . .

Works of scholarship and books of reference usually classify *In a Lonely Place* as film noir. 'Film noir' was a term coined by French critics and cinéphiles and then picked up by Anglo-Americans to describe a number of American films in the 1940s and 1950s that seemed to take a dark ('noir'), cynical attitude toward the aspirations of their heroes. Usually crime films, the films noirs show people trying, by whatever means, to get ahead in modern America and ending up betrayed, trapped, crushed. When they aren't destroyed physically, the noir film's central characters frequently suffer a moral wounding: having been slapped in the face by the worst life has to offer, the noir character becomes a hardened, bitter loner, frequently seen at the end of the film wandering the streets of the city, unable to call any place home, unable to take inspiration from any higher purpose. For many critics, John Huston's 1941 film *The Maltese Falcon* sets out the model: in a world of moral insecurity where no one can be trusted, where everyone tricks everyone else, one man, a detective, searches for truth and finds only lies and deceit. Although it obviously pains him to the core of his soul, Sam Spade turns in the murderous woman he loves and, although this act re-establishes justice, it is obvious that Spade will remain a tortured man, wounded in his heart by the treacheries of love and hardened in his outlook by the cruelties of human greed.

Typically, critics point out, the films match the dark outlook of their plots with a morally dark *style*. The visual universe of the film noir is one of sharp immersions of the world into an engulfing obscurity as shadows invade the clarity of the screen. Noir cinematography often involves single sources of light furtively cutting through a thick darkness. In the bleakness of the night, solitary street lamps beam down sharp, isolated rays that glisten against puddles of water. In seedy hotel rooms, naked light bulbs swing back and forth, throwing in and out of shadow a lone and lonely figure, lying brooding on a bed. In obscure, cluttered back alleys, noir heroes cringe against a dangerous world, their faces cut in half by the shadows or so swallowed up by the darkness that little still indicates their existence other than their eyeballs trying to pierce through the night.

At first glance, *In a Lonely Place* would seem readily to fit the film noir mode. Its main stars, Humphrey Bogart and Gloria Grahame, have become icons of the sort of film we associate with noir. Humphrey Bogart's face, for instance, with its downward pull and its beaten and bedraggled aspects, combines the toughness of the noir hero's initial ambition with the sadness and fatigue of the same hero after he's been through it all – lived all the lies, the corruption, the tricks and treacheries that the world can dish out to him. (As *In a Lonely Place* director Nicholas Ray said of Bogart, 'He was much more than an actor: he was the very image of our condition. His face was a living reproach.')

And the story the film puts Bogart and Grahame into has many of the trappings of noir: the big city at night, a city of chance encounters where each turn of the corner can spell random violence or deception or the surprises of love. *In a Lonely Place* has tough guys, tough gals, street-smart cops. It's got loads of betrayal. The film is filled with all sorts of losers and loners. Not for nothing did one of the important establishing essays for the American study of noir, Janey Place and J.L. Peterson's 'Some Visual Motifs of Film Noir', frequently use *In a Lonely Place* as a key example of the genre: from shots of curious characters looming malevolently over others to shots of amorous couples thrown off-centre by unbalanced compositions, *In a Lonely Place* easily lends itself to an analysis that looks for a style of paranoia, upset, a coherent world rendered confused and chaotic.[2]

The opening shot behind the credits of *In a Lonely Place*, reproduced in Place and Peterson's article, already seems to signal that we are in a tough world. In the dark of the night a man drives in the city, but this is shown to us in striking fashion by an emphasis on his eyes staring back from their reflection in the rear-view mirror. One could argue that this is archetypically noir: night, the modern city, the seeming confidence of forward motion combined with the undoing of confident progress by a paranoid looking back, the almost cubist fragmenting of the image into several planes (the body of the man in one place, his eyes in another). Not for nothing, too, did many reviews at the time of the film's release fully situate it within the genre of crime or urban violence stories and then often criticise it for being of this type. Take the review in the French magazine *L'Ecran français* (13 June 1951), at the time of the film's release in France: 'Once again, a film of violence, of blood and of cops. ... There are in the film as many fights as any fan of gratuitous violence might wish, as many cynical grins, car chases or eyes filled with blood as is possible. There are cops – good ones and bad ones, as expected – token drunks and several vamps. We've seen too many films of this type.' Even more extreme in its reduction of the film to basic crime elements is the contemporaneous catalogue entry on the film from the 'Union française des offices du cinéma éducateur laïque', an organisation concerned with the Christian possibilities of film as moral education: 'A well-made film but very artificial as a "série noire". As its setting: bars, nightclubs, car chases. As its action: fights, cries of terror. Moral value: nil.'

One may wonder if such descriptions are really appropriate to *In a Lonely Place*. It seems rather that a pointed choice of terms enables these critiques to assimilate *In a Lonely Place* to the crime film genre and then to criticise it for the very assimilation they themselves have effected. Look, for instance, at the individual elements these critiques find in the film. Cops: true, there are cops but they are not really so present that one might imagine this to be a standard cop-and-criminal story. As one writer on the film, James W. Palmer, notes:

> Anyone viewing *In a Lonely Place* solely as a murder mystery will surely be disappointed. Dix Steele all but solves the case twice – once when he recreates the murder for the Nicolais [the cop Brub and his wife Sylvia], and a second time when he meets Kesler [the boyfriend of the victim] at the police station and, in front of Brub, calls Kesler Mildred's jealous lover and the most logical suspect. Near the end of the film, the police discuss the fact that Kesler, after attempting suicide, has confessed to the murder. The case is resolved off-handedly and off-screen. In Hitchcockian terms, the murder story is simply this film's MacGuffin.[3]

In fact, almost to signal its distance from such a genre, the hero Dix Steele proposes to the cop Brub that they unite to find the criminal, and for a moment it seems that the film might take off in the direction of a Sherlock Holmes-like investigation – but only for a moment since the idea of an investigative team made up of Dix and Brub never re-emerges in the film.

Beyond that, what about the notion of good cop/bad cop? The usual implication is a reference to police corruption or evil (as in Nicholas Ray's next film, *On Dangerous Ground*), but in *In a Lonely Place* there is nothing of that. True, there's a friendly cop (after all, he served under Dix in the war) and a less friendly one, but both are fully professional, going about their necessary business of catching a strangler. And what about the idea that there are vamps in the film? True, the two love interests in Dix Steele's life – his former girlfriend Fran and his new girlfriend Laurel – seem women who are wise to the ways of the world, women who want success and glamour. But they seem far from vamps. Indeed, at a beach picnic with Brub and his wife Sylvia, Dix and Laurel can joke about the Hollywood woman out only for money, and their joking works to contrast that sort of woman with Laurel herself, out to get the best for herself but believing that the best can include deep and honest and pure love.

And for all the noir elements in the film, it is as easy to note how it lacks this or that element commonly associated with the form. To take a minor example, the film lacks the complicated flashback structure of many films noir – a structure that students of noir see as increasing the sense of confusion (see for instance the 1946 film *The Locket*, with its flashbacks within flashbacks) or as enframing the characters within in an inescapable destiny (since we know already how an action will turn out; see for example 1946's *The Killers*, with hero Burt Lancaster killed in the first few moments and with most of the rest of the film a series of flashbacks to explain how he got into this situation). The closest *In a Lonely Place* comes to a flashback are the superimpositions over Laurel's face as she sleeps, which repeat various warnings she's had about Dix's violent temper. But far from enclosing the character in an inevitable fate, the superimpositions increase the ambiguity of the future – will Laurel quit Dix or not? – and suggest that her destiny is not yet decided.

Even more, the familiar visual traits that scholars see as one of the defining characteristics of film noir seem few and far between. True, the opening shot of eyes in a rear-view mirror seems to partake fully of the confused, bitter universe of film noir; but as a credit shot, this image has a special status, separate from the body of the film. True, in a later scene (central to Place and Peterson's analysis), the composition is not balanced and harmonious when, on an evening out with Laurel, Dix suddenly feels himself entrapped by the surveillance of the cops; but it really is so only for a fleeting and relatively inconsequential moment. And one could note that Place and Peterson's description of the scene is in any case not fully accurate: 'Bogart and Grahame experience a rare moment of safety and security. This shot cuts to this upsetting two-shot [tight on Dix and Laurel] as the policeman who has been trailing the couple walks into the bar. Two characters each in tight close-up convey intimacy being invaded.' In fact, the cut takes us from a balanced shot of the couple to a shot of them in close, romantic intimacy (Dix asks Laurel if she still needs anything to make her happy and she leans over to whisper sensually the response in his ear), and only then do we cut to the cop coming into the bar. To be sure, the second shot in this triad does not correspond to classical notions of balance, but it avoids this to suggest a deeper, more intense harmony between the two lovers.

Indeed, the most visually paradigmatic noir moment – Dix's face thrown into menacing half-shadow as he tells Brub and Sylvia how Mildred might have been killed – is a fairly artificial moment where the stylistic flourish (a bold lighting effect) announces itself so explicitly that it can seem to stick out like a sore thumb and turn back against the thriller genre (I've had students laugh at the obviousness of the technique at this moment). Just as Dix's bursts of violence disturb the calm of his world and force people to try to interpret him, so do the film's own bursts of noir moments stand as intrusions whose status seems ambiguous.

'Dix's face thrown into menacing half-shadow'

While not ignoring the bleakness of its unhappy ending or the downbeat tone of its concern for murder, one could, without too much perversity or too much distortion of the facts, argue that *In a Lonely Place* bears as much connection to screwball comedy as to film noir. (And some screwball comedies themselves can get awfully violent and even demonstrate a callousness about death every bit as cynical as that of *In a Lonely Place* – see, for instance, the casualness with which the characters in the 1940 Hawks film *His Girl Friday* treat the suicide attempt of a young, naive girl, passed over with no more attention than murder victim Mildred Atkinson gets in *In a Lonely Place*.)

. . . .

Screwball comedies flourished in the 1930s and 1940s as parables about the ups and downs of married life. In one typical variant of screwball, a couple is split up (whether by external causes or by internalised doubts about the marriage) and, knowing intuitively but correctly that the love hasn't really gone out of the relationship, the abandoned party plots and connives to get his/her lover back (see *The Philadelphia Story*, *Mr and Mrs Smith*, *My Favorite Wife*, and so on). In a second variant, an energetic and even outrageous person recognises in a member of the opposite sex kindred qualities that are being crushed by bourgeois respectability and schemes to win the kindred soul away from respectability into a world of madcap adventure. Both forms of screwball have some overlapping elements. They represent the achievement of love as the result of tactics, of games in which one calculates ways to win over the other (and in which overtures may be blocked by temporary rebuffs). As narratives that portray love as carefully enacted plot, they seem appropriately set in urban environments – the city as the site where innocence has been lost, where even something as supposedly intense and immediate as love can only be constructed through tricks. As city stories, the screwballs are fast-talking, wise-cracking films. A famous line from Raymond Chandler's noir novel *The High Window* could equally apply to screwball comedy, where lovers also circle and stalk each other 'with the clear innocent eyes of a couple of used car salesmen'.

But even as they announce themselves as worldly-wise stories of big-city life, the screwballs eventually hold out the promise of final innocence – love as something pure even if one has to engage in impure tricks to achieve it. One way the screwballs imagine this final innocence is through a plot development in which the characters absent themselves from the streets of the big city and end up in nature: in the purity of the country (or a country-like space), the lovers can discover or rediscover the love they seemed to have lost under the pressures of city life. As philosopher Stanley Cavell argues in his book on screwballs, *Pursuits of Happiness* (Harvard, 1981), the screwball narrative often recounts the move to a 'green place' where the cares and pressures of work can be cast aside and love and festivity bloom. Today, in films like *Green Card*, we can see traces of the screwball tradition: two people from different ways of life discover flirtation mixed with suspicion and scheming in the fast world of the big city but can convert this into moments of purified, true love in special 'green places' (a greenhouse within the apartment; a rooftop away from the crush of streetlife; a restaurant named Africa, representing a world other than that of the Occidental big city).

Most immediately, *In a Lonely Place* has much of the wisecracking approach to love that we find in the screwballs (for instance, when Dix tells Laurel they'll have dinner together, she replies that certainly they'll both have dinner, but not together). This man, this woman, have each already learned many of the complicated lessons of love in the big city, and each approaches the other with interest but also wariness. The locales of the screwball film could as easily be those of *In a Lonely Place*, concerned as it is with the vagaries of love in the fast-lanes of the big city: expensive restaurants, snazzy nightclubs, apartments with comfortable couches and full bars. In such a showy world, love is a kind of staking out of positions, a reconnoitring in which one advances, checks out the situation, sends out a few feelers, and then retreats to plan strategy. And in the ways Laurel finds herself both rising in the ranks of Hollywood when she falls for Dix – hobnobbing with agents, dining with hotshots – and leaving her cheap world for one of high artistic value – quoting Shakespeare, taking on some of Dix's aesthetic inspiration – *In a Lonely Place* also echoes the screwball film's feeling that resorting to tricks and strategies in matters of love is justified if they bring the loved one out of a limited way of life.

Like the screwballs, *In a Lonely Place* imagines there is a special place where strategies can finally be put aside, where love can explode in all its joyous intensity. But where the screwball generally imagines a journey to a privileged green place outside the city, *In a Lonely Place* chooses as its special site the apartments of Dix and Laurel and the courtyard between them (a kind of green place, with its fountains and landscaping). In the Patio Apartments, Laurel and Dix can try to retreat from the world, losing track of time in a brightly lit, perfect universe. Here their love duet can proceed and recede, step by step.

The universe Laurel and Dix construct for themselves really isn't perfect, however, and isn't invulnerable. *In a Lonely Place* finally and obviously is not a pure screwball comedy. Into the green place come people to disturb their private affair (for example, Brub comes to ask Laurel to return to police headquarters), and their own doubts begin to unbalance the achieved stasis of romance. Yet one could also ask if the screwball's construction of perfect love is itself really all that perfect. The very fact that screwball happy endings are so miraculous (suddenly a couple that has been bickering all through the movie falls in love again) suggests that the screwball comedy doesn't necessarily hold out love as a pure, inevitable, necessary part of life. Whether they have happy or unhappy endings, *In a Lonely Place* and the screwball comedies, like film noir, offer meditations on romance in which it is made clear that whatever love is achieved comes at great cost, is fragile, could easily have flipped into its cynical opposite.

. . . .

'I was born when she kissed me; I lived a few short weeks while she loved me; I died when she left me.' Floating between film noir and screwball comedy, *In a Lonely Place* is one of the cinema's most intense dissections of the violence of romantic relationships, of the things men and women do in the private realm. Indeed, without pushing things too far, it might be interesting to relate *In a Lonely Place*, not to the crime story, but to a tale of violent passion like Nagisa Oshima's *Empire of the Senses* (1975). In both films, an amorous couple tries to find a special place in which to pull back from a complicated world that keeps crashing in on them: the special places in the two films even have a degree of spatial similarity (a series of rooms round a central courtyard) and, uncannily, one form of the outside world's intrusion is virtually the same in both cases (cleaning women who want the lovers to leave so that they can clean up after them). In both *In a Lonely Place* and *Empire of the Senses*, the stakes of love keep getting higher and higher as violence tunnels its way into the relationship and as the inflicter of violence has to keep asking the partner to keep faith in the intensity of love. Where the films most differ in this reading is in the Japanese film's belief that even the most violent, most fatal forms of passion represent a positive value; *In a Lonely Place*, in contrast, sees the violence as a dangerous contamination of romance's potential purity. Even more, the film raises the possibility of this contamination being inevitable. From Dix and Laurel's first embrace – in which his declaration that 'Now I know your name, where you live ... ' seems as much a menace as a declaration of romantic commitment – to its tragic finale, *In a Lonely Place* gives us few glimpses of successful romance.

By the end of the 1940s it was getting harder for Hollywood to sustain many of its driving myths. One of the most important of these myths had had to do with the supposedly redemptive qualities of love and romance. In the 1946 film *It's a Wonderful Life!*, for instance, we learn that if George Bailey had never been born, Mary 'Bailey' would never have found true love and would have ended up as a dismal old maid. So much had Hollywood insisted on the radiant perfection of the marital unit that it tried to sustain the mythic image not only in the filmed stories it offered but also in the off-screen tales it told of the personal lives of the stars and other Hollywood leading lights. Not only did Hollywood make films of perfect love, film-makers themselves seemed to want to find perfect love and, according to publicity releases and fan magazines, they usually achieved it.

Take the case of director Nicholas Ray and budding actress Gloria Grahame. They got to know each other when Ray directed her in the 1949 film *A Woman's Secret*. She was already married. They had an affair, she got pregnant, she divorced her husband and married Ray. But as Bernard Eisenschitz shows in his comprehensive biography of Ray, the Hollywood publicity machinery presented a more benign version of this potentially scandalous path to marriage; Ray was said to have met Grahame after her separation, and the period of her pregnancy was altered to fit the details of this revised version. But the fiction was only able to go so far. By the time they were working on their next film together, *In a Lonely Place*, Ray and Grahame were no longer in love. While working together on the set, they had separated in private life. Now a very different kind of fiction was needed to explain why they no longer went home together after a hard day's work: claiming that he needed to give all his attention to the film's production, Ray moved into a room on the set and tried to make the film crew believe nothing was wrong. Only much later was the couple's divorce announced in the press (Grahame was eventually to marry Ray's own son by a previous marriage!).

In the Hollywood and the US of the late 1940s, marriage and family were not inevitable, were not automatic and natural happy endings. A series of factors had rendered the myths of marriage and family life vulnerable. The war had created a situation where public duty and devotion to a cause had been promoted as superior to the private desires of the couple. A novel like Norman Mailer's *The Naked and the Dead* or stories like Edmund Wilson's *Memoirs of Hecate County* and controversial studies like the Kinsey Report had demystified love by emphasising its physical over its spiritual aspects, insisting that sexual expression could occur (according to Kinsey, often did occur) outside marriage. The postwar period had given a new legitimacy to divorce as the hasty marriages of wartime all too often revealed their fragile basis: men and women frequently found that their partners did not live up to the fantasies of sudden romance.

．．．．．．．．．．．．．．．．．．．．．．．．．．．．

In reality, and in the films of the American 1940s, men and women often wonder about each other – wonder about the intensity and purity of love, wonder about potential dangers. Film noir's frequent version of this has an innocent or principled man running the risk of being seduced into a dangerous (and often fatal) way of life by a 'spider' woman: whether he is actually a detective or not, the noir hero takes Woman as something to suspect, an object of enquiry. In so far as *In a Lonely Place* deals with a man's suspicions of a woman and with a vulnerable man's insecurity in his dealings with an evidently sexually experienced woman, the film has vague resonances of film noir. But obviously, the dangers for Dix are much less significant than those confronted by Laurel, who has to wonder directly if the man in her life is a murderer.

In this respect, just as we have seen *In a Lonely Place*'s affinities with screwball, it might also be productive to treat the film as a late example of another 40s genre, important for its thoughts on love and suspicion in the amorous couple: the female Gothic film, in which a woman wonders about the designs upon her of the man in her life – does he love her, does he hate her, does he wish to do her harm?[4]

As established with the highly influential adaptation of *Rebecca* by Hitchcock in 1940, the first female Gothic films tell of innocent and often socially average women leaping into fantasy-propelled marriages with mysterious, brooding upper-class men who spirit them off to exotic or luxurious habitats far from the big cities and everyday work the women have been used to. In the new locale, the women begin to have suspicions about the intent of these husbands who are virtual strangers to them. Where the green place of the screwball film represented a site where love could bloom magically away from the pressures of workaday big city experience, the green place of the Gothic film reveals itself as the locale in which the man's malevolent side emerges, where he is no longer held back by the compromises of the civilising process.

While *Rebecca* precedes America's entry into World War II, many later female Gothic films may well be a response to postwar conditions. For example, the film woman's growing suspicion of the man parallels that of the real postwar bride whose sudden romantic marriage gives way to discontent when the husband returns home and turns out to be different from her dream of him. The widespread early postwar discourse (in magazines, newspapers, films, therapeutic manuals) on the maladjusted, even psychotic, nature of many returning veterans perhaps helps fuel a suspicion of men who come from an exotic elsewhere to bring aggression into the marital sphere. But in the postwar moment – in the moment of Kinsey and a new fictional awareness of sex and passion – there is also a reworking of the female Gothic genre in which the menace for the woman is not that of an exoticness intruding into ordinary life but, on the contrary, of a deadeningly dull emptiness coming from the man and threatening to crush the new sensual energy of the woman. It is appropriate that the end of the 1940s saw a Hollywood production of Flaubert's *Madame Bovary*, treated as the ultimate tale of a woman defeated by the boredom of the everyday. Such Gothic films chronicle the deceptions that ensue when a passionate woman encounters a trivial world which has little time for her passions.

It is easy to see *In a Lonely Place* as a late and modified manifestation of the female Gothic tradition. Laurel is, like the Gothic heroine, a figure of ascension, the ordinary woman picked out of the crowd to become something more (at one point, Dix even tells Mel that Laurel would be perfect for the part of Althea Bruce). But entry into the world of privilege means also a realisation of its foibles and corruptions and dangers. Discovering, like the second Mrs de Winter in *Rebecca*, that her man has a mysterious, even dangerous past (including another woman, Dix's dark-haired former lover Fran), Laurel must work to understand the man, must make him a target of constant interrogation. (As with the second Mrs de Winter, Laurel's suspicions are given intense visual rendition by a scene in which she tosses and turns in bed while voice-overs enumerate the terrible things about her man's past.)

As critic and science-fiction writer Joanna Russ says of the heroine's fears in the Gothic novel: 'In one way the Gothics are a kind of justified paranoia: people *are* planning awful things about you; you *can't* trust your husband (lover, fiancé); everybody's motives *are* devious and complex, only the most severe vigilance will enable you to snatch happiness from the jaws of destruction.'[5] As in the Gothic, where the heroine finds that even the special place in which she encounters her man is itself mysterious (as in *Rebecca*, with its dark hallways and closed and locked rooms), menace comes to Laurel in the form of a living space rendered malevolent: the window an enraged Dix peers through, the doors he bangs at and crashes through, the stairway on which they frequently play with each other and down which he flees at the film's end after he comes close to strangling her. And as with the typical Gothic heroine, much of Laurel's suspicion manifests itself as *reactive* worry and wonder and not as an active attempt to do something forceful about her doubts: in Russ's words, 'The heroine's suffering is the principal action of the story because it is the only action she can perform'[6] – and Laurel's passive suffering is even amplified by the fact that her suspicions of Dix lead her to take sleeping pills and become drowsy.

....

Faced with a woman who is losing her love for him, Dix becomes ever more possessive, wanting to know of Laurel's every action and demanding to be in charge of her life at every moment. And such fictional domination seems to have had its real-life counterpart. As an article by Edwin Schallert in the *Los Angeles Times* (4 December 1949) recounts:

> So rare is the husband-director and wife-star combination in Hollywood that Gloria Grahame had to sign a special agreement with Producer Robert Lord to be a nice girl when she was cast opposite Humphrey Bogart in the picture, 'Behind the Mask', formerly 'In a Lonely Place', which her spouse Nicholas Ray was to boss on the film set at Columbia. Whether because of this pact ... or because they get along well together [!], there has so far been no cataclysm in the Ray household or at the studio. 'The main thing that the agreement required is that I obey my husband,' said Miss Grahame. I thought I detected a slight trace of acid when she said the word 'obey' but she disarmed me by smiling ... she admitted that she has been hewing to the line of her agreement.

According to Vincent Curcio in his biography of Gloria Grahame, *Suicide Blonde*, Ray arranged for a loan of Grahame from RKO (from which he himself had been loaned) but as part of the deal arranged this private contract giving him full professional control over everything she did, from 9 to 6, six days a week.[7] Uncannily, many of the film's recognitions of the violence and domination of the modern male and of the difficulties of love in the contemporary world seem to have found an echo in details of the film's production. (Even the name of the actual killer, Henry Kesler, comes from the name of the film's Associate Producer, in a strange in-joke.) Whether art is imitating life or life imitating art, the backstage production of *In a Lonely Place* seems as much to enact 1940s tensions in male-female relations as do the developments of its plot.

Screenwriter Dix Steele has elements both of Humphrey Bogart and of Nicholas Ray: the character, Steele, in fact lives in the first apartment that Ray had when he arrived in Los Angeles. Ray and

Bogart lived lives that blended passion and violence and rendered their relations with women chaotic, bitter and violent. Ray's own misogynist recollections at the end of his life capture some of this:

> Bogart and I shared levels of experience in common with each other, but there must have been something else. We were both married to younger women, he to Bacall, I to Grahame, and they were near to each other in age and pregnancy. ... Both were talented actresses who worried about the same wrinkles, the twenties wrinkles. Each was promiscuous, Gloria by far the more offensively so. Each had her own style, but Bacall's was elegant, and she was the more intelligent of the two. Grahame schemed better and on a lower level.

In a curious event that might almost have been a publicity stunt (but wasn't), just one month before production began on *In a Lonely Place* Bogart was charged with an act of public violence at New York's El Morocco Club which was almost identical to Dix's several outbursts at

Nicholas Ray directs Bogart and Grahame

Paul's Restaurant (and we might note that the film at one point mentions the El Morocco). As *Variety* recounts it, on 28 September 1949, 'According to the early stories, the star had shoved a girl who tried to pat one of a pair of toy pandas which the actor and a friend, Billy Seeman, had seated at a table with them in the nitery at 3.30 a.m. The girl, a pretty model, went sprawling on the floor and Bogart was admonished by El Morocco management never to darken its zebra stripes again' (Bogart had also been banned from the Stork Club, also mentioned in the film).[8] Charges against Bogart were eventually dropped and, in a climate where Hollywood had been getting bad press for a number of antics by 'bad boy' actors (for instance, Robert Mitchum and Robert Walker), the publicity machine did what it could to keep the story quiet.[9]

Interestingly, Lauren Bacall concludes her account of the incident in her autobiography, *Lauren Bacall By Myself*, by claiming that Bogart could never engage in violence, but follows this up with an admiring mention of his desire to exert control over women:

> Bogart hailed the decision [dismissal of the charges against him]. ... The reason Bogie never got into any real trouble was that his derring-do was always innocent. He just didn't like hurting people. No wonder he was everyone's hero. All through our life together, the most fun was where he was. ... Bogie had a joke dream – that a woman should be able to fit into a man's pocket. He'd take her out, talk to her, let her stand on the palm of his hand, dance on a table, when she got out of order – back in the pocket. And she could be made life-size when desired.[10]

. . . .

If we follow the vagaries of the production history of *In a Lonely Place* we again encounter a variety of versions of romance. Just as the film of *In a Lonely Place* seems to offer one version of the love story pulled from a larger typology (which ranges from *Empire of the Senses'* affirmation of passion to the Gothic's sense that passion is out of place), so did each version of *In a Lonely Place*, from novelistic idea to filmic realisation, seem to test a series of possibilities in the rendition of violent love.

In a Lonely Place was very vaguely based on a 1947 novel by mystery writer Dorothy B. Hughes.[11] She took her title from J. M. Synge's 1903 play *In the Shadow of the Glen*, about a woman isolated in the Irish highlands who rejected her violent husband. Hughes prefaces her novel with a quotation from Synge about people's desperate need to reach out to others across isolation: 'It's in a lonesome place you do have to be talking with someone, and looking for someone, in the evening of the day.'

Anyone turning to Hughes's novel after the film is in for surprises: there are quite major differences between the novel and its screen adaptation. A study of these changes can help us understand the particular logic of the film by pinpointing the narrative choices that were made for it and seeing how they fit into the film's overall structure. In this case, a novel governed by one set of rules – coming from a thriller framework and geared to tunnelling inside an obsessive mind – gives way to a film made from very different rules, rules which open up the individuals in its story to complicated encounters that blur social and sexual interaction.

Born Dorothy Belle Flanagan in 1904 in Kansas City, Hughes began her writing career as a journalist and poet before achieving her primary critical success as a writer of mystery and thriller fiction, starting in 1940 with *The So Blue Marble*. Three of her thrillers from the 1940s were adapted by Hollywood: *The Fallen Sparrow*, *Ride the Pink Horse*, and *In a Lonely Place*. Hughes's first novels were international conspiracy thrillers, some clearly influenced by Hammett's *The Maltese Falcon*. In *The Fallen Sparrow*, *The So Blue Marble*, *Johnnie* and *The Black-Birder*, the hero or heroine comes into possession of a centuries-old treasure and then has to fend off menace by all sorts of eccentric characters who will do anything to get the treasure for themselves. Written under the shadow of war in Europe, these novels set up a conflict of all-American protagonists against decadently aristocratic Europeans (or Europhiles) and have the average Yank heroes succeed through a combination of their own ordinary and commonsensical knowhow and determination *and* an appeal to forces of law and order (local police plus government crime-busting and spycatcher organisations).

Several qualities remain constant in Hughes's novels of the early

1940s. Obviously, as thrillers, all play on crime and paranoia; in particular, the central characters fear, and fight against, webs of entrapment that slowly but unavoidably close in on them. What is particularly striking about Hughes's novels in this period is less this general paranoia (which we can also find in, say, Cornell Woolrich, another thriller writer whose works were frequently adapted for the screen) than the specific narrative style she employs to give this paranoia body and intensity. Although none of her 1940s novels is directly in first-person, the narration sticks very closely to the central character as he or she moves through a world of menace, reads the clues of that world and wonders about them. The opening of *Dread Journey* is typical: ' "I'm afraid." She had spoken aloud. She hadn't meant to; she hadn't wanted those words to come up from her throat to her lips. She hadn't meant to think them, much less speak them.'

Significantly, in light of the serious recognition that the film of *In a Lonely Place* gives to a woman's point of view, Hughes does not seem a writer much concerned to give women power in a narrative. In, say, *The Fallen Sparrow* or *Johnnie*, we seem clearly to be in the hard-boiled universe of cynically world-weary men trying to survive the treacheries of, among others, cold-hearted vampirish women. While in novels such as *The So Blue Marble* or *The Black-Birder* or *The Cross-Eyed Bear*, the central figure is a woman and the novel's narration glues itself closely to her point of view, this is a powerless point of view in which we see the woman suffering the consequences of a menacing world closing in around her: the heroine seems unable to do much to fight the evil conspiracy threatening her and often has to wait for a superhero to show up to rescue her (for example, a globe-trotting, fast-talking, hard-drinking macho ex-husband in *The So Blue Marble*).

While it maintains the highly personalised third-person narration of the wartime novels, the postwar *Ride the Pink Horse* (1946) would appear to signal a significant shift in Hughes's writings that prepares the way for *In a Lonely Place*. Like the earlier novels, *Ride the Pink Horse* is set in a world of organised conspiracy, of professional crime and corruption, with a protagonist trying to survive the evil doings closing in around him, except that in this novel he is himself a criminal (a gangster in the pay of a corrupt Chicago senator) and will himself become a murderer (of a cop) by the end. The personal third-person narration functions here both to further the paranoid plot (will he live or die?) and, unlike the earlier novels, to offer a portrait of the mind of a criminal (and one, like Dix in *In a Lonely Place*, who finds his cold violence tempered by the love of a woman).

With *In a Lonely Place*, the thriller framework of organised corruption is left behind. Like Jim Thompson's cult classic *The Killer Inside Me* or Bret Easton Ellis's notorious *American Psycho*, *In a Lonely Place* is a psychological portrait of the lone psycho-killer as he goes about his gruesome business. There is still a third-person narration that glues itself to a central protagonist's point of view. There is still the overriding concern with this protagonist's awareness that a web of entrapment is drawing ever closer. But the protagonist is now a deranged murderer, and the web of entrapment is no longer an evil external conspiracy but comes alternately from his own anxieties and the mistakes they lead him to make, or from the forces of law enforcement as they do their grim but necessary work.

Even if one isn't interested in judging whether *In a Lonely Place* the novel or *In a Lonely Place* the film is better, it is easy to feel that in the case of this Hollywood adaptation the film-makers have found ways to create a work that is as rich and complex as its source. In the novel, for example, Dix Steele is a fiction writer but has been supported by his rich uncle to the extent that he doesn't really need to work at all. In fact, in the novel it is never clear to what extent Dix really is a writer or just uses that as an excuse, to isolate himself by claiming that he needs time to write or to ask Brub questions about the murder of Mildred on the ground, that it's for novelistic research. The one time in the novel that Dix actually sits down at his typewriter, he does so to write to his uncle for more money. In contrast, the film's emphasis on Dix as a literary artist forced to betray his talents for money gives an additional twist to the pathos of his entrapping personal life. The movie's Dix Steele is trapped as man and as worker in the meshes of the Hollywood system. As much as he would like to imagine himself part of an aristocratic leisure class with time to write creatively, the film's Dix is an industry employee smarting under the restrictions the Hollywood system places on him.

Indeed, as is often true for films directed by Nicholas Ray, *In a Lonely Place* shows a very precise attention to milieu and its immediate, and often constraining, effects on character. In contrast, while Hughes's novel is set in Los Angeles, it is not a Hollywood novel and makes little mention of film production (the novel's Laurel has no real aspiration to be in the movies since, as she says, she'd then have to get up early). In another novel, *The Davidian Report* (1952), the author makes clear her sense of Los Angeles as the opposite of the constraining system of bosses and workers that is so evident in the film version of *In a Lonely Place*. Hughes's Los Angeles is just another city: '[Steve] took his time walking back to Hollywood Boulevard. Not much of a boulevard. … mostly the street was home-towny, an overgrown Main Street. It was probably why Hollywood Boulevard had become a lodestone. Any American, except perhaps a born New Yorker, would feel at home on it. … Unlike its sister back streets of New York, this one was near to deserted. No housewives squabbled amiably … no children ran under heels into the traffic. There was no traffic, not even a passing car. Nor was there curiosity evinced in a stranger, and he well knew a stranger was as recognizable in this isolated sort of community as on a village green.' Los Angeles here is simply a neutral, benign backdrop.

Hughes's version of paranoia seems much less environmental than psychological: what one has to fear is what is in one's own head (hence the constant recourse in her novels to a point of view that, even though rarely a literal first-person narration, stays with the central protagonist and processes events through his/her perception and analysis of them) or in one's emotionally loaded relationships with others. Typical in this respect would be the opening of *In a Lonely Place*, where Dix stands on a bluff in a blanketing fog over the Los Angeles beaches, reflects on his situation and then goes stalking after an unknown woman who appears out of the swirling dark of the night. The fog here is part of a dematerialisation of external reality that leads Hughes to focus instead on inner thoughts: the novel's Dix could be a killer anywhere (and indeed he has been: he killed a girlfriend while on war duty in England).

In contrast, critics have commented on a sociological or ethnographic bent in many of the films of Nicholas Ray. *Rebel Without a Cause* is adapted from a non-fictional book on delinquency, and the film keeps much of the original concern with a socially defined problem. Other Ray films, such as *Hot Blood* (on gypsies) or *Wind Across the*

Everglades (on bayou trappers), are concerned with the everyday life and particular foibles and dreams of a distinctive subculture (and in this respect we might add the portrayal of Jesus and the Disciples in *King of Kings*); and at least one film – *Savage Innocents*, about Eskimo life – is explicitly ethnographic in its close look at the patterns of a particular culture.

From the focus of his first film, *They Live By Night*, on two young lovers separated from a normal world by an inescapable descent into crime, Ray films often deal with members of a group isolated from mainstream culture by a difference in life-style and morality, by rituals of inclusion and exclusion (for example, the 'chicken run' in *Rebel Without a Cause*), by specialised codes of behaviour and practices of language, by rites and personal myths. The dramatic relation in the films is not just of characters to each other (although Ray's films are also inspired by a deep romanticism which makes person-to-person encounters often intensely charged with the *Hot Blood*, whether violent or amorous, referred to in that film's title). It is as much a relation of characters to a world around them, whether a world they reject, or one that has rejected them, or one into which they seek (hopelessly) to be integrated.

The film of *In a Lonely Place* has a sociological or ethnographic aspect not present in the book. It is not so much a story of a psychotic killer as a depiction of a whole subculture and its mores. As much as anything else, *In a Lonely Place* is a Hollywood narrative, joining in a tradition of depictions of that world that range from the fictional (Nathanael West or F. Scott Fitzgerald or Norman Mailer) to the non-fictional (for instance, Hortense Powdermaker's ethnographic *Hollywood, the Dream Factory*, whose cataloguing of the hierarchies and conflicts of Hollywood power parallels that of *In a Lonely Place*).[12] While we are never on the set, or even in a studio, in *In a Lonely Place*, Hollywood is a pervasive force in the lives of these Los Angeles people. We see their preferred eating places, we learn about the industry's hierarchy and its typical members (from the acclaimed but talentless director to the aging agent, the producer who succeeds by nepotism, the has-been, or the hangers-on like Mildred, all too interested in going home with a screenwriter to be part of the movie-making process). The film's decision to make Dix Steele a screenwriter contributes to an essential thematic conflict not present in the novel. As a writer, Dix is a figure of culture, the possessor of higher aesthetic values in a world dominated by aesthetically inferior beings. If much of his sympathy is for the Shakespearean actor who himself failed to sustain artistry in a money-hungry industry, it is also obvious that such sympathy is a doomed gesture – that this new world is going to push the artists and intellectuals out of the way to make room for forces of banality and triviality (for example, Junior, the man Dix fights with at the film's beginning, a figure of the new Hollywood who has forgotten the creative legacies of the past).

Most immediately, these inferior beings are quite simply the masses, the people, members of the ordinary and everyday world. They show up as the various ordinary guys Dix confronts out on the road and gets into fights with, but the image of a tasteless public is especially incarnated in the hat-check girl Mildred, the film's epitome of vulgar, lowbrow anti-value. At first Dix seems mildly amused at Mildred, and there's even a hint of sexual interest in his taking her home. Yet in a way that suggests *In a Lonely Place*'s parallels (and the parallels of many tough postwar films) to the Existentialist ethos in France at the time, any passion for the ordinary material world can easily turn into revulsion or dismay or simple sick weariness at it (what Jean-Paul Sartre calls 'nausea'). When Dix realises fully how ordinary Mildred is, he quickly sends her away (sealing the crass materiality of the encounter by giving her some money), and the next time he and we see Mildred she has more than re-entered the realm of the material: she is now a corpse, nothing but inert matter, and with a bluntness that seems a bit surprising for the Hollywood cinema of the refined classic era the film shows us pictures of her death, her body little more than a lumpy physicality thrown alongside the road like a bulky sack someone desperately wanted to get rid of.[13]

Indeed one writer on Ray, Stefano Masi, goes so far as to argue that even if Dix turns out not to have been guilty of the murder of Mildred, symbolically he could have been, that the murder is a projection of the aesthete's own desire to strike out at a vulgar world he wishes to rise above. In Masi's words, 'Oscar Wilde would have loved *In a Lonely Place* for its excessive sensibility, for the completely Elizabethan tone of its mixing-up of theme and form and for its ordinary

LIBRARY

The opening scene: Dix in a random encounter

LIBRARY
COLBY-SAWYER COLLEGE
NEW LONDON, NH 03257

characters with their aspirations toward something superior. *In a Lonely Place* would have particularly pleased Wilde because of its morbid interrogation of art and life.' For Masi, the film narrates how Dix's elitist aggressions are carried out for him by someone else: the Wildean metaphor of a life imitating art is 'projected onto a writer who, not able to express himself, explodes his own violent creativity against the world that surrounds him. Reality, in return, materialises a phantasm of the writer; that is, it interprets his own contempt in the confrontation with Mildred and realises it.'[14]

In the depiction of a divided Dix, the very opening of the film is illuminating in the way several of its incidents very economically signal the fundamental contradictions that will drive Dix on. In short succession, for example, we see Dix quoting Shakespeare with a has-been actor and then turning instantly from man of culture to man of violence when the alcoholic actor is mocked by another Hollywood denizen (Junior). Most revealing is the virtual repetition of one of Dix's earliest lines. In the very first scene, Dix stops at a traffic light and, in one of the random encounters of everyday city life so common in tough postwar film (encounters that equally hold out the mystery of new friendship and romance and the menace of chance aggression), he first chats with a woman who announces herself as an actress in one of his films and then exchanges verbal barbs with her husband. When the vocal sparring threatens to turn into a fight (the husband telling Dix to pull his car over to the kerb), Dix answers, 'What's wrong with right here?' (in other words, in the middle of the street). Only a few moments later, Dix says virtually the same thing. But now the context is different. In Paul's restaurant to meet his agent and a successful director, Dix takes them to the bar for a drink. When the director spies the alcoholic has-been, he suggests moving to the other end of the bar. Sympathetic to the drunk's plight, Dix replies, 'What's the matter with right here?' On the one hand, Dix as figure for whom the only thing that matters is using violence blindly in any tension-filled situation; on the other hand, Dix as cultivated man who stands up for the rights of the underdog.

Between the two scenes – Dix in his car, Dix in the restaurant – there is a scene of transition as Dix moves from outside into the restaurant and, at the door, is asked by some young kids for his autograph. One of the kids advises another that Dix is a 'nobody', an evaluation Dix agrees with. On the one hand, this description of Dix is amplified by the subsequent dialogue – in which we learn he hasn't had a hit screenplay in a long while – and suggests that Dix's sympathy for the down-and-out Shakespearean might revolve around an affinity among losers. On the other hand, it is obvious from further dialogue at the bar that Dix doesn't really consider himself a loser; for instance, he implies that the director's financial success is based on repetitive exploitation of the same story and thus is no real cultural success at all. And even before Dix reaches the bar, a minor scene in which he looks with a mixture of disdain and disbelief at an overdressed and vulgar woman asking for matches from Paul's suggests that his real feeling is one of superiority rather than inferiority.

Dix is a special figure moving through a vulgar world. If he can accept the nomination of 'nobody', this term is to be taken as a sort of zero-degree marker, Dix's status as an ambiguous figure who can either stay above the corruptions of the world (and thus stand up for culture, as with the Shakespearean actor) or be tempted to embrace them (and thus turn into a violent fighter, as with the husband in the car). We

'What's the matter with right here?'

might note that the film is deliberately ambivalent about the cause of Dix's violence. For example, we are told early on that he is a war veteran, and the scene at Brub's house where Dix demoniacally describes how you strangle someone suggests an explanation in the mythology of the returned soldier as psychotic, a common image in popular film and literature of the postwar period. Then there is a suggestion that Dix is working out the aesthete's disdain for the ordinary world, a disdain he manifests as physical aggression. And there is also the implication that the violence comes from Dix's own inability to resolve the question of just who he is: man of culture, average guy.

As a screenwriter, Dix is immediately caught up in a nexus of power that means he is never really able to be his own man. When he tells others near the beginning of the film that he might someday write something really good, we realise that his writing talent may not be so much something he has as something he aspires to: if he is so concerned to defend a myth of high culture in the mass culture world of Los Angeles, this may be in part because he is not so sure that he really merits high-culture status himself. In the film itself, we never see evidence of Dix's talent; rather, we hear Dix and others endlessly declare that he has (or has had) such talent.

Ambiguities abound. Take, for instance, Dix's script. Early on, Dix seems to regard the novel on which it is based as trash that is beneath his talents, and later when Mel asks Laurel (who's been typing Dix's adaptation) how well Dix has been following the book, she looks worried and evades the question, thereby confirming that Dix is writing something quite different. Even later, Mel tells Dix that the script is no good because it doesn't follow the book. But given all these seeming indications of Dix's uncompromising drive to write his script his way, what are we to make of the fact that producer Brody is said at the end of the film to have loved Dix's script? All along we've been told that the only adaptation that would please Brody would require Dix's sell-out, and now we're told that Dix has perfectly met Brody's desires for the adaptation. Dix, it is said, is 'in'.

I hope the question of Dix's potential talent doesn't seem like those old-fashioned questions in literary criticism where, treating characters almost as real people, one wonders how many children Lady

Macbeth had, and so on. There, one has to imagine off-stage details, to treat the characters as if their lives extended beyond the fictional space. The question of *In a Lonely Place* seems to me different, since it is in relation to what's happening on-screen during the running of the film that the issue of the character's artistic ability arises. For instance, much of what we tend to like in Humphrey Bogart as an actor might seem to contradict the image of Dix as aesthete: Bogart's aura as actor connects to an image of a man who is worldly, not artistically above that world – a man who is physically tough and streetwise, not an artist cloistered off in a world of creativity.

And if the casting of Bogart as Dix Steele renders ambiguous the image of Dix as high-culture artist, the casting of Gloria Grahame as Dix's muse, Laurel Gray, also confuses the issue. For the ostensibly artistic Dix, Laurel is supposed to represent the ultimate artistic inspiration, the ultimate impulse to creativity. And yet it is hard to see this in the film (the quotations from Shakespeare seem as strange coming from Grahame as they do from Bogart). As Grahame plays the role, there's a lot of earthiness, even ordinariness, even perhaps vulgarity in the character. Alain Ménil's comments on Grahame as Laurel are apt: 'There is in her an astonishing mix of elegance and "cheapness", which makes her a star of derision. ... She can incarnate to perfection the girl from nowhere who goes forward to meet her fate, having already thrown overboard all illusions and hopes.'[15] This is not to say that Grahame is wrong in the role. Quite the contrary, she seems to be a perfect match for Dix Steele as played by Bogart, a Bogart with the earthy qualities we associate with him and whom we might well imagine attracted to this kind of woman in this kind of world.

The question of Dix's talent is also essential to the issue of the sexual politics in the film. Throughout, characters around Dix excuse his violence because they regard him as a special and privileged being. And some critics have echoed these alibis for Dix's aggressive nature. Jean Wagner, for example, seems to believe that Dix deserves more sympathy than the murder victim Mildred:

> What can be done in this world – in particular, in a world as superficial as that of the cinema – by an individual like this who seems to be revolted by everything of life, pleasures, ugliness,

beauty – who seems to apprehend existence as if it were a limitless galaxy, as if the Absolute inhered in the smallest gesture, the smallest word? What's admirable in Nicholas Ray is that he succeeds in convincing us that there is only one possible attitude: to hit one's fists against everything in reach. If we find Dix somewhat crazy, he is one of those magnificent fools for whom we would gladly exchange many normal people. It's to him that one almost wants to give anonymously the flowers that he reserves for the poor, murdered Mildred.[16]

But if Dix is not a special being, if his talent isn't proven, even this curious defence of the violent male becomes hard to sustain. One might profitably compare *In a Lonely Place* with its portrayal of the aspiring writer whose inspiration tips into violence to Kubrick's *The Shining*. Putting a man and a woman together in an isolated, enclosed space in which suspicion grows, both films start from a seemingly fixed genre (noir, horror) to move instead toward a domestic melodrama that suggests an origin of male violence in a personal failure that the man refuses to admit.

A further change from the original novel has to do with point of view. Although the novel is written in the third person, its point of view always stays with Dix: what he sees, hears, feels is all we know, and information about the people and the world around him is channelled through a narration of his feelings and reactions. In contrast, while in many scenes in the film the narrative point of view seems to be adhering fairly closely to Dix's point of view, it also frequently diverges from it.

Even the very opening of the film is revealing in this respect. The opening shot, under the credits, simultaneously gives us a point-of-view shot from Dix's perspective and a perspective on him: we are in (or very close to) the driver's seat of the car Dix is driving, and we see the road before him as he does, but we also see his eyes reflected in the rear-view mirror. As with the novel, we have here a point of view that is simultaneously first and third-person. But as the credits run, cuts intercede and the camera moves back away from the car so that we view the whole vehicle from a position external to Dix. The film has quickly become even less his point of view, and in the next scene, in Paul's restaurant, cutaways to the commentaries of other diners suggest that Dix's isn't the only experience to matter, that everyone has his or her point of view in and on the Hollywood world. Even more, they have points of view about Dix: for example, after his tussle with the vain actor, there is a cutaway to a woman commenting on the fact that Dix is at it again.

Some of this wandering of the point of view away from Dix is, to be sure, in keeping with a general theme of the original novel. In the novel, Dix wonders if the cops are wondering about him (and by the end of the book we discover that they were), and the film maintains this image of Dix as an object of scrutiny and investigation by showing us scenes of police investigation. But in the film such inquiry is not simply judicial, not simply undertaken by the police because they think Dix is a murderer. Dix is also investigated, thought about, studied by people for reasons that are personal and even sexual. In particular, he is an object of inquiry by women, especially by his prospective lover Laurel. Several scenes show Laurel away from Dix, reflecting with friends and acquaintances about him and his potential for violence. The film is not

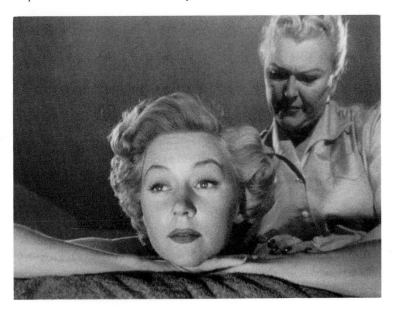

Laurel and her masseuse, Martha

just about Dix but also about a woman's growing suspicion about Dix.

Moreover, several scenes of Laurel with other women discussing Dix hint at a special solidarity among women that sets itself up against male control. Sylvia, for example, tells Laurel to give no account to Lochner's suspicions (even though Lochner is her own husband's boss). An early version of the screenplay even has Sylvia declare, 'Luncheon is such a wonderful excuse for men to talk about their business, and for women to talk about their men.' But the most pronounced moments of woman-to-woman intimacy are Laurel's scenes with her masseuse Martha. Martha actively dislikes Dix, fuelling Laurel's fear by spreading stories about his past violence, and she resents his intrusions into her private encounters with Laurel. Although the script gives her a son at UCLA, she is played according to 1940s clichés of butch women, and the film implies a special bonding between Laurel and Martha.

With Laurel, women wonder about Dix. And even before it makes Laurel an active figure, *In a Lonely Place* shows a concern to portray women's perceptions of men, or more precisely of this man. As

Dix with Mildred

we noted, the opening of the film (where he is seen by a woman he hasn't noticed) evidences a point-of-view structure that doesn't limit itself to Dix's perception. This bypassing of Dix's perspective continues in the next sequence when Dix leaves with Mildred and takes her home. In the novel, Mildred is no more than a figure who gets off a bus, is seen by Dix, walks home, and is then strangled. The film's Mildred, in contrast, is given a complex identity (the first close-up of her coincides with her announcing her name, and she is soon telling us about her life with the aunt she lives with) and, even more, she is given a degree of autonomy by the editing which portrays her apart from Dix and wondering about him.

Much of our shock in discovering Mildred's death comes from her independent vitality, from the energy of her performance, and from the sense of her as a full person given her own narrative weight in the first moments of the film. Thus early in the scene in Dix's apartment, the editing gives us shots of Dix alone in one room slipping into something more comfortable, alternating with shots of Mildred hearing his shoes hitting the floor and wondering about his motives. Dix here is an object of inquiry as much as an inquirer. Even as the film emphasises Mildred's low-class background (she is prone to malapropisms, such as calling a microscope a 'microbe' or saying that a risqué novel is 'risky'), it also invests her with a warmth and a whimsy (as the lively Mildred exits from Dix's apartment and from the film, the music goes into a spry motif, giving no indication of her fate).

Indeed, from the beginning, the film sets up women as figures who look at and thereby interrogate Dix. Some of the incidents are minor in themselves, but they fall into a pattern whereby Dix is turned into an object of scrutiny. Thus where the novel begins with Dix seeing a woman get off a bus and spying on her, the film begins with Dix noticed by a woman he doesn't notice (the actress in the car with her husband). In the next scene, in the restaurant, a former lover comments to others on Dix's propensity for violence. In the following scene, Mildred wonders about his intentions, and then, after a scene in which Dix is interrogated by the police, Laurel is introduced and the inquiry into Dix as man continues. In the police station Laurel sits with her back to Dix, and one of her most pointed actions is to turn round and look significantly (but ambiguously) at Dix when Captain Lochner tells

4 2   An interrogation and a challenge: Laurel's pointed looks at Dix in Captain Lochner's office

her Mildred Atkinson has been strangled; she turns round again and looks pointedly when Dix clarifies the mode of strangulation. My interpretation of this scene differs, then, from British critic Geoff Andrew's analysis in his *Films of Nicholas Ray*. Following other commentators who regard Captain Lochner as 'bad' in his drive to track down the murderer at all costs, Andrew takes Laurel's act of looking at Dix (and away from Lochner) to indicate her shift of allegiance to Dix away from the pressuring of the police:

> Looking operates on one level ... as an index of preferential loyalties, a function further demonstrated when Laurel is first brought in for questioning by Lochner; seated facing him, with Dix (whom she has never properly met) positioned behind her, she looks at Lochner until told that Dix is suspected of murder, at which point she turns around to study Dix's face. Trapped between the men, she is forced to choose which to believe; having decided that Dix is innocent, she then sits looking at him rather than at the cop who, to gauge *her* trustworthiness and regain her loyalty, is then forced to cross the room to position himself next to Dix. None the less, his efforts are fruitless, since Dix and Laurel have made contact; although they answer Lochner's questions, they continue to look, act, and address their replies to each other.[17]

Now it is true that there is a battle of allegiances. As Laurel answers Lochner's various questions about Dix and about her evident interest in him, it becomes clear that through her answers she is also engaging in the first steps of a love duet with Dix. But I think they are nothing more than the first steps: when Laurel tells Dix the next day that she has decided she's interested in pursuing things with him, my impression is that we have to assume that *this* is her moment of unequivocal commitment and not the earlier moment at police headquarters. In Lochner's office, Laurel seems to me still to be sizing up Dix, and her gaze at him is an interrogation and a challenge, as much as a commitment of amorous allegiance.

In the novel, Dix looks and is fascinated. In the film, women look at him as much as he does at them; for example, when Dix peers for the first time out of his apartment window at Laurel's apartment, he finds her on the balcony looking intently back at him. In the first encounter with Laurel, she had simply been a passing figure, cutting between Dix and Mildred as they headed toward his apartment. Dix had seemed entranced by this passing spectral figure and turned back to look at Laurel several times. This is like the obsessive Dix of the book, but in the film Dix quickly loses control of this sort of captivated gaze. For example, in the apartment with Mildred, there is a curious shot when Mildred looks directly into the camera and talks; nominally, her object is Dix, but a reverse shot reveals that he is not even looking in her direction. The forcefulness of this shot of Mildred – a violation of the often important injunction against the look at the camera – gives the woman's look an intensity that suggests that Dix's observational power is not the only one in play in the film. As Geoff Andrew says of this scene, 'When Mildred summarises the book for [Dix], Ray has her speak directly to the camera, which (mirroring Dix's wariness) pulls backwards, only to watch her step forward again, into almost oppressive close-up.'[18]

44   Dix finds Laurel looking back at him

But in this respect, the greatest change between novel and film is quite astounding: in the Hughes novel, Dix turns out to be the serial killer the police have been after. Hughes's novel is a fascinating glimpse into the mind of a psychotic, and even though it's written in the third person, it stays with Dix at every moment, narrating his fears and desires, revealing no more than what he perceives or knows.

The cliché about Hollywood films as betrayals of their literary sources often bases itself on a charge of moral or aesthetic cowardice on the part of Hollywood film-makers, their concern for making money supposedly leading them to avoid all that is challenging or scandalous in literature. But in the adaptation of *In a Lonely Place*, the major change of Dix from killer to simply violent man doesn't just result in establishing the innocence of a leading character played by a popular star (like Cary Grant in *Suspicion*, where it was impossible to make him a murderer). Quite the contrary, even as the film acquits Dix of the already committed murders, it quite emphatically shows his potential for murder and his capacity for everyday violence, especially against women. Even more than a murder mystery in which socially deviant

Dix's 'potential for murder'

figures attack the culture from the margins, *In a Lonely Place* shows a violence installed within the heart of the dominant culture, ready to break out at any moment. Indeed, the film's acquittal of Dix as the murderer sought by the police has as one obvious consequence that someone else has to be guilty of the murder of Mildred. In another change from the novel, it turns out that Mildred's own boyfriend, a seemingly mild-mannered clerk, strangled her. Murder here is something that all men can be suspected of with justification; there is no limiting of the potential for violence to one social group (even the middle class has its murderers) or to one form of aberrant psychological disposition (Mildred's boyfriend is not a psychotic, and Dix often seems to be able to hold his own violent urges under rational control). Even the decent cop Brub gets into the act when, at Dix's encouragement, he starts strangling his wife during an attempt to act out the probable details of Mildred's murder. One could easily read the film as a proto-feminist work that argues that men *per se*, not this or that murderous man, can pose a threat of violence to women.

Dorothy Hughes did not seem to mind that her novels were transformed. In a discussion of publishers' modifications of her books, she claimed, 'It's like having a book made into a film or TV script – certain changes are necessary as they are different mediums from book writing, and who am I to criticise the experts in their fields?'[19]

From novel to first adaptation, second adaptation and last-minute on-set modifications, *In a Lonely Place* offers a virtual typology of the forms of guilt and innocence. Significantly, none of the versions tried for a happy ending in which Dix and Laurel might end up together.

. . . .

In a Lonely Place was the third film from independent production company Santana Pictures. Santana had been created on 7 April 1948 by Humphrey Bogart, former Warner Bros producer Robert Lord, and Bogart's business manager A. Morgan Maree, and named after Bogart's yacht. Originally, the company had been an initiative of former Warner producer Mark Hellinger, a friend of Bogart's who had bought a number of properties (including *Knock on Any Door*, the first Santana production) in anticipation of full-studio independent production. But Hellinger died suddenly in 1947, and Bogart bought up his stock and properties, becoming President of the company.

There had been a big drive in the 1940s toward independent production, encouraged by a number of factors.[20] Changing economic and organisational conditions – such as government attacks on the block-booking system in which big studios would force theatres to rent blocks of as many as thirty films (often sight unseen) – favoured a one-by-one production of films rather than an assembly-line approach. With the postwar break-up of total studio control over theatres, and with television making consumers more choosy in the spending of their entertainment dollars, it became advantageous to make fewer films and give greater care to qualities that might differentiate one film from another. For example, the publicity for independent productions sometimes focused on a creative individual, such as a director, to give a film an aura of special prestige (this was the case for instance with Fritz Lang's films for independent producer Walter Wanger).

But it wasn't only a claim of artistic excellence or diversity that gave incentive to independent production. If film personnel could separate themselves from studios and form private corporations, they could frequently work out new tax possibilities that allowed them to get away with paying much less to the government. (This may have been of special concern to Bogart – in 1949, the Treasury Department found him to have been the film industry's highest paid actor; and *In a Lonely Place* has a line about a film-maker who was lucky enough to amass his fortune before the introduction of income tax in the 1940s.) In addition, independent production often gave creative personnel a sense of freedom from companies they long felt had oppressed them (even if they eventually came back to those very companies, as was the case with another independent, James Cagney). In a revealing statistic in her article on independent production, Janet Staiger notes that the number of members of the Screen Actors Guild under exclusive studio contracts dropped from 742 in February 1947 to 463 a year later. Bogart in particular appeared to have chafed under Warner control, and Santana was a virtual Declaration of Independence for him from the Warner monarchy. Indeed, one Bogart biographer, Allen Eyles, claims that Santana tried to get a loan-out of Lauren Bacall for the part of Laurel Gray but that Warner Bros was so annoyed by Bogart's new independent status that the studio refused.[21]

But even if it seemed a slap in the face to this or that studio, independence only went so far. (And we might note that Bogart was still under contract with Warner Bros during the period of Santana Productions; he had simply negotiated a contract that allowed him one independent production per year.) A feature film-maker might break from any single company, but it was necessary to form some alliance with one of the major companies to gain access to distribution networks and to financing possibilities (unless there was private financing, as for instance David O. Selznick had with multi-millionaire John Hay Whitney). Santana had a deal with Columbia Pictures (the first studio to which Bogart had ever been loaned) in which they provided distribution and studio space for the shooting.

As tax laws were changed, as audiences proved unpredictable for many of the experiments of independent production, as the studios themselves found new ways to incorporate diversity into their own productions (see, for instance, the big studios' exploitation of the youth film in the 1950s), it became obvious that independent production was a surefire guarantee of very little. Some companies lasted for only a film

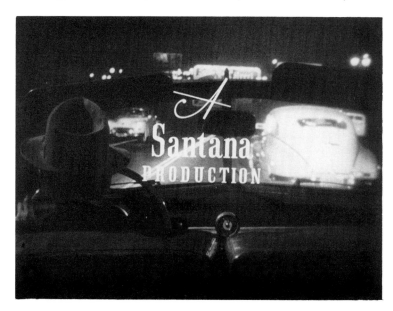

or two. Fates fluctuated. In an article in the *New York Times* on 27 October 1948, Santana was already declaring that *In a Lonely Place* might be its last production, while by 1 June 1949 *Variety* was announcing five new projects of the company. In such fluctuations and in the constant move of independent companies to and from big studio alliances, one can see the ambivalence that *In a Lonely Place* itself dramatises about independence: Dix Steele wants both to work on something he can be artistically proud of and to succeed financially in a system which requires that success entail compromise and submission.

....

Dix's 'I want it, I don't want it' attitude was also that of director Nicholas Ray. Simultaneously, Ray wanted to experiment with the rules of Hollywood storytelling and rebel when those rules constrained *and* to endorse the studio system as the only context possible for feature film-making.

Ray was born in small-town Wisconsin in 1911. His early years seem to have been characterised by a deliberate aimlessness (youthful rebellion, adolescent alcoholism and so on). After some experience with radio broadcasting during high school, he spent a year at the University of Chicago but didn't exert himself and left abruptly. However, a professor he had often partied with – the writer Thornton Wilder – thought enough of Ray to recommend him for a fellowship at architect Frank Lloyd Wright's intellectuals and artists colony, where Ray came into contact with some of the freshest thinking in American artistic and cultural experimentation (including new modes of 35 mm film projection). It is difficult to say what precisely Ray gained from his time with Wright, although some scholars suggest that his later fascination with a symbolics of space and with CinemaScope and its ability to facilitate striking compositions organised horizontally may have been inspired to a large degree by Wright's model of architecture. Political differences seem to have led to a split between Wright and the more leftist Ray, and the young man left for New York where radical theatre was enjoying its golden moment of the 1930s.

Ray became a member of a theatre collective, the Theater of Action, a company in which every member spent long hours in training (mental and physical, political and dramaturgical) and learned all aspects of theatrical production. Through his work in the theatre, Ray made a number of contacts with the artistic and intellectual community of New York – most importantly a friendship with Group Theater director Elia Kazan, who also directed for the Theater of Action. In his biography, Bernard Eisenschitz suggests that Ray gained from the Theater of Action a concern with the power of sharp contrasts and striking juxtapositions (theorised under the name of 'montage') and from the Group Theater a fascination with the powers of deeply passionate acting.

Ray's experience with theatre led to his being asked in 1937 to join the theatrical branch of the Special Skills division of the Resettlement Administration (a government agency concerned with housing the displaced poor of the Depression). Believing that cultural production was important to the building up of American morale, the Resettlement Administration (like many other government agencies of the time) included a strong commitment to the arts, and Ray found himself in contact with other artist members of Special Skills such as Ben Shahn, Jackson Pollock and Pete Seeger. The most important association, though, was with Alan Lomax, who was working on a project of recording American folk-music for the Library of Congress. Ray joined the project and contributed to Lomax's famous discovery of important singers from marginalised subcultures, for example the rhythm-and-blues singer Leadbelly. On the basis of this work, Lomax was recruited by CBS to produce a radio show of American musical forms and he engaged Ray as an assistant. When the Second World War broke out, Ray's radio experience led to his joining John Houseman's Overseas Branch of the Office of War Information, concerned with promoting American values around the world. But political pressures claiming that the OWI was too partisan and even too left-leaning led to a crackdown on operations, and Ray and Houseman were forced out.

Meanwhile, Ray's old theatre buddy, Elia Kazan, had been called to Hollywood on the basis of some Broadway successes. Beginning production for 20th Century-Fox of *A Tree Grows in Brooklyn* (1945), Kazan got the studio to hire Ray to direct screen tests and to work as assistant director; Ray appears to have used the experience to learn as much about movie-making as possible. He was called back to New

York by Houseman and made his directorial debut on an early TV movie, *Sorry, Wrong Number*. When Houseman went back to Hollywood, where RKO had him under contract, he took Ray with him.

Ray was finally allowed his Hollywood directorial debut in 1947 with *They Live By Night*, a story of young lovers on the run adapted from a novel by Edward Anderson, *Thieves Like Us*. Shooting on the first day the first action of the script – a thrilling jailbreak – Ray immediately gained a reputation among Hollywood professionals for daring experimentation: he filmed the first scene from a helicopter (a complicated process for a novice director on his first day on the job), and did so not just to offer a higher view of the action but to increase tension through the complicated and changing movements of camera and helicopter in relation to fleeing figures and cars.

Unfortunately, RKO went through a change of ownership and new owner Howard Hughes (who otherwise liked Ray) held up release of *They Live By Night*. Although a 1947 production, it did not get an official release until November 1949 when Ray was already in the middle of filming his *fifth* feature, *In a Lonely Place*. Nonetheless, Hollywood professionals were able to screen the film early on, and his reputation as a film-maker grew. Ray followed *They Live By Night* with a routine assignment, *A Woman's Secret* (made, it seems, so that the studio could find work for some of its actors under contract), and then was requested for a loan-out from RKO by Santana Productions to film *Knock on Any Door*, a combination juvenile delinquency and trial film (with the male lead split between young John Derek, whose motto in the film is 'Live fast, die young, and leave a good-looking corpse', and the world-weary Humphrey Bogart). After a return to RKO for the melodrama *Born to be Bad*, Ray was again recruited by Santana for *In a Lonely Place*.

In the 1950s, Ray became one of the fetish directors of a number of French cinéphiles, mostly grouped around the journal *Cahiers du cinéma*. By the 1960s, Ray was also a regular and revered object of attention for British critics in a number of little journals like the *Brighton Film Review*, *Monogram* and *Movie*. As Antoine de Baecque, one of today's editors of *Cahiers du cinéma*, puts it in his history of the early years of the journal, 'Among the "fathers", there was one whom *Cahiers du cinéma* revered above all the others: Nicholas Ray. If there were to be only one name to incarnate the cinema, it would be his. . . . *Cahiers* keep coming back to him: Ray *is* the cinema.'[22] François Truffaut's contrast of Ray's contentious position in Hollywood with Howard Hawks's more casual one captures the unrestrained enthusiasm of the French critics for an energetic American cinema:

> In Hawks, we see the triumph of the mind, in Nick Ray the triumph of the heart. One can argue against Hawks and for Ray – or the other way around; one can condemn [Hawks's] *Big Sky* in the name of [Ray's] *Johnny Guitar*, or accept them both. But anyone who rejects either should never go to the movies again, never see any more films. Such people will never recognise inspiration, poetic intuition, or a framed picture, a shot, an idea, a good film, or even cinema itself.[23]

The French critics especially seem to have been trying to work out the guilt of their evident admiration for Hollywood cinema – was there a way to love it without liking what was 'mass' in this mass cultural form? – and the idea that certain strong directors produced personal films from within the Hollywood system was a way for them to resolve this ambivalence. In these terms, Ray seemed a perfect choice. Making films which often centred on rebels, marginals and otherwise unique figures, Ray himself seemed to cultivate an image as rebel. On many of his films he fought with the producers; he was replaced as director in several cases, and often complained that the final version of his films differed greatly from his original conception and execution. For the French critics, Ray seemed to encapsulate what they enjoyed in American cinema – its energy, its vitality (interestingly, one author of a book on Ray, Jean Wagner, is also a jazz critic) – but he also represented the critique they felt American culture needed. French critics found in Ray's films a reflection of the pressures of family life, the crush of social conformity, the dangers of mass thought.

Ray's comportment helped in the construction of him as an auteur. Beyond the fact that he was a hard-living rebel, he also cultivated an image as intellectual artist, as a thinker. On the one hand, he talked to the Europeans of authors they knew (on several occasions

Ray talked of making a film of the life of the poet Rimbaud) and of themes dear to their cultural tastes, such as the existential crisis of the individual. As Jean Wagner puts it, 'One cannot look at Ray's heroes without thinking of [Camus's] Mersault.'[24] On the other hand, the very fact that Ray talked with the critics, that with intelligence he made explicit his artistic goals and desires, allowed them to feel that he was not so far from themselves. One senses the delight of the editors of *Sight and Sound* in their 1961 interview with Ray when they discover that, far from the typical Hollywood mechanic or slave or hack, he turns out to be a person of ideas and even of explicit programmes that bridge the gap between artists and critics:

> He speaks slowly, as though he were chipping his sentences off some rough block of ideas, knocking his thoughts into shape as he goes. Talking about his own work, he is self-critical, absorbed; he is concerned about what people think, concerned especially about clarity, the way an idea communicates itself on the screen. ... [In the realm of criticism] he would like greater definition of terms, would like the critic to set out the standards in evaluating a film, then to meet the director on the ground of a specific picture which could then be analysed by critic and director according to their separate lights. This would be a fascinating laboratory exercise, and one hopes it can be realised.

Whether or not they come from Ray's personal obsessions (and if they do, whether their presence in the film marks his genius), there are in *In a Lonely Place* a number of the preoccupations that fans of Ray find in all his films: an intense, almost claustrophobic centring of much of the narrative on a single protagonist in his or her (but usually his) encounters with the world; an intense relationship between two men, one usually older and the symbolic guardian of the other (here, the relation of Dix and his agent Mel); an equally intense relationship (what Jonathan Rosenbaum nicely refers to as a 'duel and duet') between a man and a woman where the possibility of love is held out as a chance for redemption from a cruel world; the intrusion of outsiders for better or worse into the love 'duel and duet' of the couple (here, the scene where Mel looks on as Laurel and Dix tussle romantically); an inner torment that bursts out in sudden and unexpected paroxysms of love or passion or both; sudden shifts of tone (here, for instance, the transition from the lightness of Dix's evening with Mildred to the cold shock of her death announced the next morning); the insufficiency of the family to sustain the individual; a fascination with genre hybrids (a gangster musical like *Party Girl*, a women's film that is also a Western like *Johnny Guitar*; here, the very difficulty of deciding what *In a Lonely Place* is: murder mystery? love story? film noir? Hollywood exposé?); empty 'happy' endings or even ambiguously open endings; lives lived on the edge (*On Dangerous Ground*, as the title of one Ray film has it); special places offered as sanctuaries against a crushing world (here, the apartment complex itself as a place of inspiring love); night as the moment where energies run high (*They Live By Night*, according to the title of Ray's first film); a strong sympathy for marginal figures and social outcasts (here, the drunk; even the close-ups given to black singer Hadda Brooks fit with the frequent concern in Ray films to give attention to excluded groups and their forms of cultural expression); beyond this concern with specific marginal individuals, a larger ethnographic interest in depicting the everyday life of cultures other than that of the typical American spectator (Eskimos, Bayou trappers, low-life criminals, rodeo riders, juvenile delinquents; here, the bigwigs of Hollywood and their various servers, assistants, followers and sycophants); members of the ordinary world as a virtual folk chorus (in Greek tragedy style) who judge the actions of the protagonists and even move on to active persecution (hence the recurrence in Ray films of lynch mobs, posses and so on; here, the commentators in the background in the opening nightclub scene; Ray's concern with persecution might also be seen in Lochner's persistence in investigating Dix down to the smallest detail).

....

Ray's loan-out to work on *In a Lonely Place* went into effect in August 1949. The start date for the production was 25 October and filming was planned to run until 5 December.

There is some confusion about who did what on the script for *In a Lonely Place*. The credits list screenwriter Edmund North as having done the original adaptation from Dorothy Hughes's novel, and another screenwriter, Andrew Solt, is given final screenplay credit. No one seems to have considered North's treatment very important for the final film. Born in 1911, North had a long career in scriptwriting, alternating genre pictures (for example *Colorado Territory*, a rewrite of *High Sierra*) and stories with artistic pretension and even social ambition (soon after *In a Lonely Place*, for instance, he scripted the jazz tragedy *Young Man With a Horn*, which he envisioned for black actors, and the liberal anti-hysteria parable *The Day the Earth Stood Still*). He eventually won an Oscar (with Francis Ford Coppola) for his contribution to the script of *Patton*. In the 40s he had freelanced, working on both independent productions (*Dishonored Lady*, 1947) and studio work (for example *Colorado Territory*, 1948). The comment in Bertrand Tavernier and Jean-Pierre Coursodon's encyclopaedic *50 Ans de Cinéma Américain* seems accurate: while declaring that they find North's work to have been 'relatively underestimated', they admit that 'It is true that he is often the only name in the credits and it is difficult to know if his work was respected or disregarded.'[26]

It is generally assumed that North's version of *In a Lonely Place* was a short treatment of the film that followed the book closely. Andrew Solt claimed that he was never shown this version and told Bernard Eisenschitz that it was probably written early on when Santana were thinking of *Knock on Any Door* star John Derek for the story's young psycho-killer. According to Solt, the North version became irrelevant when it was decided to drop Derek and reconceive the role for an older Dix Steele who would not turn out to be a psychotic serial killer. An additional factor in moving away from the original story may have had to do with the Production Code Administration, the office for enforcing moral codes for film. In his research on Bogart's films, film historian Robert Sklar found correspondence from producer Robert Lord promising Code director Joseph Breen that there would be no attempt to represent the evil doings of a serial killer: 'We intend to have the protagonist kill only one person within the framework of the story. He has killed another person before the story begins.'[27] Lord's reference to a killing 'before the story begins' is intriguing. Is the reference to the novel's Brucie (Dix's first girlfriend and victim), killed before Dix gets to Hollywood, or to Mildred Atkinson, killed before the main story of Dix and Laurel gets going?

Edmund North died in 1990. His widow Colette North did not remember *In a Lonely Place* as having been a major job of her husband's and imagines that the treatment was simply a routine assignment. In an interview with the Oral History Program at U.C.L.A., North himself said he remembered little about *In a Lonely Place* except that he wrote a treatment which the film-makers decided not to use. He appeared to have no regrets at all about this. In any case a second scriptwriter, Columbia regular Andrew Solt, was assigned to write a new script for the picture. Born in Budapest in 1916, Solt was a budding playwright when he was brought to the US in the 1930s by a Hollywood talent scout. He began as a scriptwriter for Columbia (his biggest film was *The Jolson Story*, 1946), but by the end of the decade he was also regularly writing for independent productions (most famously, the Ingrid Bergman film of *Joan of Arc*, 1948). Just before *In a Lonely Place*, he had worked on another thriller/woman's picture, *Whirlpool* (which also recounts the falling apart of a love relationship under police interrogation).

By the time Solt came on board, it had been decided that Bogart would star in the film. Solt's version had to offer something very different from the original plot of the Dorothy Hughes novel. Three months were given over to the writing of the script, and Solt had regular input from Lord and Ray. The final script is dated 19 October 1949, and a shooting schedule was typed up on 18 October, a week before the start of the shooting, suggesting that there was little space for modification. Indeed, in interviews and in public lectures Solt claimed that the narrative of the filmed version follows his script very closely. His story is that Bogart liked the script so much that he demanded not a word be changed in shooting. According to Solt at a presentation of *In a Lonely Place* at a Columbia Pictures retrospective at the Los Angeles County Museum in 1984:

> I was asked to Bogart's house to read the script to him. Present were Bogart, his wife Betty Bacall, and Nick Ray. ... By the time I turned to page ten, I knew the script worked. ... When I finished reading there was a long silence. Betty fixed me a stiff drink but said nothing. Since she had no part in the film her presence was that of the star's wife. Nick Ray, I knew, was on my side. It was all up to the boss. Bogie took a long drag on his

cigarette, holding it in the famous Bogart fashion. ... Then he
said, 'It's okay. We'll make it as is.'

But Bernard Eisenschitz's careful research proves that this is simply not
the case. As he notes, the late date on the final script may indicate
simply that plotting details were being worked out up to the last
moment. Indeed, Eisenschitz's research reveals that the film's script was
still being revised even late into production. As he says, 'Of the 140
pages only four made it to shooting *without* revisions.'[28] Eisenschitz
goes on to explain that while these changes might seem to have come
from Solt (probably in consultation with the others), even Solt himself
admitted that he was not present during the actual shooting. According
to Solt in his Los Angeles presentation, he dared, at the first reading at
Bogart's house, to suggest how Bogart should prepare for the role:

> I was too drunk with success. 'To make this story work the
> camera must move even closer than the usual close-up shots of
> your face – it must photograph your brain!' He took another puff.
> I was still unaware of his icy expression. ... 'It's well known that
> you never learn your lines the night before. ... With this script
> that won't work. This time you must study your lines and analyse
> them and know them before you come on the set.' Betty couldn't
> watch my Hungarian hari-kari any longer. She interrupted me
> and led me to the door. Bogart kept his word. The script was shot
> virtually unchanged. But I was barred from the Presence. Nick
> Ray made me understand that Bogart didn't want me on the set.

Most of the revisions and changes seem in fact to have come from Ray
in consultation with Bogart and Grahame. Indeed, Ray's copy of the
script includes handwritten modifications that suggest last-minute
changes even on the day of shooting. Significantly, in light of what I
said earlier about Ray's contractual control over Grahame, most of his
handwritten notes have to do with directions for her. Ray seems to have
given particular attention to perfecting the image of Laurel Gray's
growing suspicion, and almost all his jottings indicate ways to give a
doubleness to her actions (an appearance of love for Dix, a reality of
doubt in him). For example, when in response to Dix's proposal of

marriage Laurel runs to the stove, crying that the coffee is going to boil over, Ray indicates in the margin her underlying worry, 'What do I do? How do I get out?'

Beyond written modifications, Ray, Grahame and Bogart worked out new dialogue and actions during the shoot. Some of these modifications don't seem to change anything central. For example, the scene of Dix being questioned by the cops originally included the presence of a stenographer, but this was changed to a hidden microphone (thus, suggests Eisenschitz, fitting Ray's continuing concern with recording mechanisms and surveillance techniques) whose presence Dix astutely guesses. Some of the changes simply improve the dramatic sense of the film (for example, Solt's final script has scenes of Henry Kesler following Mildred so that we know he is the murderer, although these scenes are not indicated in the shooting schedule and may have been dropped early on). Generally, the film tries to leave issues of guilt as ambiguous as possible for as long as possible. The script includes, for instance, shots of Dix and Laurel looking at each other after Mildred has left, while the film eliminates all of this (thus leaving open, as we'll see, the question of the truthfulness of Laurel's alibi).

Other changes are more important. For example, the opening scene of Dix's encounter with an actress and her husband – so important to setting the tone for the whole film – was added on 8 November. Some modifications seem in keeping with Ray's own preoccupations. The filmed version drops a reference by Mel to other (and younger) screenwriters he is also representing, and adds the two moments in which Dix (affectionately) tells Mel he's got to get a new tie: these seemingly minor changes render more intimate the friendship between Mel and Dix and fit Ray's concern with older man/younger man relationships.[29] Similarly, at Paul's restaurant the various cutaways to people who comment on the action (for example Fran, who says 'There goes Dix again' when he punches and knocks over Junior) are not in the script and appear to reflect Ray's interest in chorus-like figures who evaluate the main action.

The most important modification is in the ending, a modification as astounding as the changes from Hughes's novel. Solt's final shooting script finds Dix innocent of the murder of Mildred but ends with him killing Laurel. Shot for shot, the final moments of this version are almost identical with the filmed version until the moment that Dix begins to throttle Laurel. One difference allows the script version to engage in a bit of ironic poetic justice. In Solt's final typed version, the screenplay that Dix has written and which Mel takes to give to Brody (in hope of giving Dix a triumph so that he will not feel the hurt of Laurel's exit) is missing its last scene: when Dix kills Laurel, he finishes the script and brings his love life and his career to a simultaneous end (and *In a Lonely Place* also concludes at that moment). It is worth quoting Solt's script in detail, from the moment Dix is strangling Laurel:

IN A LONELY PLACE
Second Revised Page – 140
November 9, 1949

. . . .

INT. LOCHNER'S OFFICE – NIGHT

159A   MEDIUM SHOT LOCHNER AND BRUB
Brub is listening on the telephone, waits a second,
then hangs up.

BRUB
No answer

. . . .

INT. LAUREL'S LIVING ROOM – MORNING

161   MEDIUM CLOSE SHOT
Dix, in shirt-sleeves, sits at the desk, typing. He uses his two forefingers. The knock on the door is repeated. Dix looks up. There is a strange expression on his face – the sign of insanity – a more dead than alive quality. He is oblivious to the room, the world. Slowly he rises, goes to the door. CAMERA PANS with him and, for a moment, takes in the open bedroom door and what we can see through it. Laurel's body is lying on the bed, clad in the dressing gown. She seems to be asleep.

. . . .

A horrible scream is heard from the bedroom. Then another.
A second later, Martha and Effie run from the room. They
look at Dix, frightened, then run past him.

MARTHA
(turns in doorway)
You've killed her!

She runs out, following Effie. Dix sits staring at the page in
the typewriter.

EXT. BEVERLEY HILLS STREET — DAY

164A   FULL SHOT
Two police cars, sirens screaming speed past Camera.

. . . .

EXT. BEVERLEY HILLS STREET — DAY

164B   FULL SHOT   .
Martha, Effie and a few other people, probably tenants, are
standing in the middle of the garden watching anxiously as
Brub, Barton and others from the Homicide Bureau hurry up
the steps to Laurel's apartment.

INT. LAUREL'S APARTMENT LIVING ROOM — DAY

165   FULL SHOT
Dix is seated at the desk, still typing, as Brub, Barton,
policemen, a photographer and others enter the room. The
policemen remain in the door. The others go into the
bedroom. A moment later, Brub comes out, walks up to Dix.

BRUB
Hi, Dix.

Dix looks up. There is a faint smile on his face. He is glad to
see Brub.

DIX
Just a second, Brub. I'm finished.

He types a few more words, then gets up, nods to Brub.
They start out of the apartment. CAMERA MOVES UP to the
typewriter.

INSERT: PAGE IN TYPEWRITER
It is the last few lines of Dix's screenplay. They read:

CLOSE UP FAREWELL NOTE

I was born when she kissed me
I died when she left me
I lived a few weeks while she loved me.

FADE OUT

THE END

Indications are that this version was shot. A scene-by-scene shooting
schedule prepared by production assistant Earl Bellamy programmes
the shooting of this original ending for 15–17 November. And the
revised ending – the one that went into the final version of the film – is
dated 18 November, suggesting that dissatisfaction with the original
ending was almost immediate. Ray offers an account in a documentary
portrait, *I'm a Stranger Here Myself*:

I just couldn't believe the ending that Bundy [Solt] had written. I
shot it because it was my obligation to do it. Then I kicked
everybody off stage except Bogart, Art Smith and Gloria. And we
improvised the ending as it is now. In the original ending, we had
ribbons so it was all tied up into a very neat package. ... And I
thought, Shit! I can't do it, I just can't do it. Romances don't have
to end that way. Marriages don't have to end that way, they don't
have to end in violence for Christ's sake, you know. And let the
audience find out and make up its own mind about what's going
to happen to Bogie when he goes outside of the apartment area.

. . . .

Columbia's own suggestions for the promotion of the film show that even the industry itself had no one view of its theme or message. For most of their films, the Hollywood studios produced promotion booklets with suggestions to local theatres on ways to make the films saleable. In the case of *In a Lonely Place*, the pressbook shares the hesitation as to what the film is all about. The booklet reveals that for Hollywood the point of a film may not necessarily be its theme, a meaning, an ideology, even a story, but simply a number of bold attractions it can offer: 'Suspense, intrigue, suspicion, love, hate, a blonde and a man with a violent temper are a few of the many exploitable angles. Put 'em to work!' For the industry, the film is not a message but a set of saleable images that link up with a larger world of merchandising. For instance, the promotion booklet suggests that theatre-owners put lobby cards not only in their theatres but in other businesses in town: resorts, hotels or travel agencies might build a display around the question 'Care to Honeymoon in a Lonely Place?' while telephone mail order businesses might advertise by suggesting, 'If you live in a lonely place ... '

One ambiguity revolves around the issue of the generic definition of the film: is it a love story or a thriller? A display advertisement for the film blends a romantic image of the central couple in passionate embrace with the very different captions, 'Suspense in the Night', 'Intrigue at Dawn', 'Suspicion around the Clock', 'Surprise finish'. Two contests for customers bizarrely indicate the ways the studio thought of the film as a commodity open to the most contradictory of marketing tactics. First, a contest for the male spectator: we see a close-up of Bogart's eyes and are asked the following questions, which simultaneously pick up moments from the film but also work at a level of generality that the average spectator can identify with: 'Are you a man of violence? What is your reaction when you watch someone being unnecessarily cruel? Are interrupted by an unwelcome phone call? See long-anticipated plans thwarted? Are followed or watched persistently? Know your friends are talking about you? Are asked to do menial tasks? Are in an accident through carelessness? Receive unsolicited and unwelcome advice? Are prevented from acting as you choose? Suspect the behavior of your girl?' And a point-scoring system even lets us know how violent we are. Here we can see a promotion participating in precisely that sentiment in the film that all men are potentially violent and should be interrogated (by themselves or by those around them) for their susceptibility to violent impulses.

Then there are also questions for women spectators. Significantly, instead of asking women to wonder if the men in their lives are violent (or even murderous), the quizzes revolve around love as much as murder. For example, one competition shows lobby cards of Bogart in other movies staring at women and asks, 'Look deep into Bogart's eyes – is it love, hate, or murder?' Another promotion even makes these ambiguous eyes into the very object of desire: theatres are instructed to hang a cut-out of Bogart's eyes over a mirror so that women can see themselves as they see Bogart, and ask, 'Girls, would this man look at you the way he looks at Gloria Grahame "*In a Lonely Place*"?' One suggested promotion goes so far as to make love the sole issue: 'In the film Gloria Grahame is somewhat hesitant about falling in love with Bogart; she isn't sure she wants to. [Note how this renders Grahame's doubts as issuing solely from romantic questions, rather than suspicions of violence.] Ask the question: "Do blondes fall in love faster than brunettes?" Guest tickets to the best answer.' Another even uses the idea of isolation suggested by the film's titles, but again romanticises it as a desirable thing: 'Arrange for a sorority or other group of girls to name Humphrey Bogart "the man we'd like to be in a lonely place with." Fraternities might reciprocate with the choice of Gloria Grahame.' Significantly, there is no mention in the pressbook that Ray and Grahame are married (nor does this fact show up in reviews of the film). Despite what I said earlier about Hollywood's fascination with a mythology of the amorous couple – or perhaps because of this fascination – the pressbook has to hide the fact that Grahame is already married so as not to destroy the illusion of on-screen romance with Dix and so that audience members can be encouraged to fantasise their own relationship with her.

....

Of all the ambiguities and unanswered questions in *In a Lonely Place*, two are particularly striking. First, how do we evaluate the open-ended ending? From Hughes's novel (where Dix kills, and often) to the screenplay hinted at in producer Robert Lord's censorship letter (where Dix kills, but only twice), to Solt's first screenplay (where Dix didn't kill Mildred but does kill Laurel), to the version shot (where Dix kills no one, but comes awfully close to killing Laurel), we remain in a story of a man's culpability, of a potential (whether realised or not) for violence. No version ever considers Dix triumphing over his aggressive inclinations. No version tries to make things work out happily.

From the very first reviews, it seems that some viewers did not know quite what to make of this uneasy ending with no perfect couple. Critical responses range from that of *Variety* (17 May 1950), concerned as ever with the marketability of films and feeling that the ending is not 'audience-pleasing', to that of *Newsweek* (5 June 1950), reading the ending as not so unhappy after all: 'One gets the impression that the disturbingly malevolent character created had to be whitewashed in the last reel for the benefit of more squeamish moviegoers.' And the absence of a tied-up happy ending leads commentators on the film to imagine a variety of probable outcomes for Dix. For Andrew Solt (in his interview with Bernard Eisenschitz), the film is 'the portrait of a future killer'. For the *Pittsburgh Post-Gazette* (14 July 1950), 'This type of fellow in real life is not long for this world.' For Ray himself, little is certain: 'In *In a Lonely Place*, at the ending of the film you do not know whether the man is going to go out, get drunk, have an accident in his car or whether he is going to go to a psychiatrist for help. And that's the way it should be; either one of the two things could happen to him because now the pressure is off, but now there's an internal pressure.'[30]

For Ray, the important issue is Dix. Even as he wonders what Dix will do next, he feels he knows why Dix got that way. As he says in the same interview, 'In *In a Lonely Place* Bogart was under the pressure of society. Accusing an innocent man released his hostility. ... There it was a social pressure of accusation and suspicion.' The leap is not far from this to Jean Wagner's praise of Dix as an unfairly pressured superior being who deserves the sympathy held out to Mildred. But for me, the most nagging issue has less to do with Dix than with Laurel. Is she telling the truth when she testifies initially that she knows Dix is innocent because she saw Mildred leave his apartment alone? The novel has no place for such a question (since Mildred never visited Dix at all). Solt's screenplay eliminates all doubt by intercutting a scene, after Mildred's departure, of Dix and Laurel looking across the courtyard at each other.

In the film, no definite clarification. As Dix says goodbye to Mildred at his doorway, the camera pans right to follow Mildred going away. No shot of Dix looking. No shot of Laurel's looking. Fadeout. Of course, some reviewers seem to need to have the issue appear unambiguous: for *Time*, for example, in its negative review of the film (5 June 1950), 'Bogart's innocence of the crime seems so clearly indicated at the outset ... that moviegoers may wonder through a few reels what the picture is driving at.' In fact, Laurel's testimony is given no support by anything we see on the screen. That she later tells Sylvia that she's not sure Dix didn't kill Mildred would indicate that her original observations allow for the possibility that Dix could have found a way to kill the hatcheck girl.

In the exchange of looks in the police station, it would appear then that Laurel sizes up Dix and *guesses* at his innocence. In the films of a more romantic director, this initial guess might sustain the woman and lead to an all-conquering love. In many Hitchcock films, for instance, a woman feels a man's innocence and stays devoted to him, even as all the clues point to guilt (for example, in *The Lodger*). But *In a*

'I lived a few weeks while you loved me. Goodbye, Dix'

6 5

Lonely Place has little faith in love's redemptive powers. Laurel's initial leap of romantic faith in Dix is a mistake. But it's a mistake for obvious ironic reasons: Dix did not kill Mildred, and Laurel was (unintentionally) right to offer him an alibi; yet Dix could have been a killer. And in a nice detail, it is not clear why Dix stops strangling Laurel at the end. Does he suddenly realise the terribleness of what he's doing? Or does the ringing phone bring him out of his psychosis?

In the ending that Ray improvised with Bogart and Grahame, Laurel, still rubbing the skin that Dix's hands were crushing, responds to Lochner's declaration of Dix's innocence in Mildred's death, 'It doesn't matter, it doesn't matter at all.' Dix is innocent and guilty together. Laurel's reply is one of the last lines of the film. In the very last, she watches Dix wander off and rephrases his formula of doomed love: 'I lived a few weeks while you loved me. Goodbye, Dix.' Laurel, too, seems to have been born and to have died in the space of a relationship. Just as we might wonder where Dix will go next, we could also wonder about the woman's future. What is love for her now? What can it mean? This, perhaps, is one of the enduring issues we can find at work in this woman's film.

NOTES

....

1 In a nice comment on the scene, French critic Serge Daney referred to the composition as 'love in long shot'. Where a more typical means to picture the intensity of the relationship might have been to track in on the two characters, Daney suggested that the long shot creates a reverse 'movement' – 'one that passes *into the body of the spectator*'. See *Ciné-journal* (Paris: Cahiers du cinéma, 1986), p. 254.

2 See Janey Place and J. L. Peterson, 'Some Visual Motifs of Film Noir', *Film Comment*, vol. 10 no. 4, January–February 1974, pp. 30–5. Reprinted in Bill Nichols (ed.), *Movies and Methods* (Berkeley: University of California Press, 1976), pp. 325–38.

3 James W. Palmer, '*In a Lonely Place*: Paranoia in the Dream Factory', *Literature/Film Quarterly*, vol. 13 no. 3, 1985, pp. 200–7.

4 For introductions to the female Gothic genre, see Joanna Russ, 'Somebody's Trying to Kill Me and I Think It's My Husband', *Journal of Popular Culture*, vol. 6 no. 4, Spring 1973, pp. 666–91; Diane Waldman, ' "At Last I Can Tell It to Someone!": Feminine Point of View and Subjectivity in the Gothic Romance Film of the 1940s', *Cinema Journal*, vol. 23 no. 2, Winter 1984, pp. 29–40; and Tania Modleski, *Loving With a Vengeance: Mass Produced Fantasies for Women* (New York: Methuen, 1984).

5 Russ, ' "Somebody's Trying to Kill Me" ', p. 681.

6 Ibid., p. 686.

7 Vincent Curcio, *Suicide Blonde* (New York: William Morrow, 1989).

8 *Variety*, 5 October 1949.

9 See such items in *Variety* as 'Robert Walker's Arrest, After Mitchum's, Prods Action on Pub Relations' (27 October 1948) and ' "Bad Boy" Stars, Hollywood's Poor Public Relations Prompt Industry Leaders to Urge Aggressive Action' (24 November 1948).

10 Lauren Bacall, *Lauren Bacall By Myself* (New York: Random House, 1978).

11 For Hughes's own account of her move into mystery writing, see her 'The Challenge of Mystery Fiction', *The Writer*, vol. 60 no. 5, May 1947, pp. 177–9. See also the interview in *Ellery Queen's Mystery Magazine*, July 1978, pp. 122–3. For partial analyses of Hughes, see Lesley Henderson, *20th Century Crime and Mystery Writers* (Chicago: St James, 1991), pp. 578–9; Elaine Budd, *13 Mistresses of Murder* (New York: Ungar, 1986), pp. 53–63; and Victoria Nichols and Susan Thompson, *Silk Stalkings: Women Who Write of Murder* (Berkeley: Black Lizard Books, 1988), pp. 22–4.

12 Though one may wonder if it isn't Powdermaker that Ray has in mind at the beginning of an essay published in 1956: 'The innocent public has learned much about writers and producers from the drawing room anthropologist, who arrives in Hollywood for a short visit and a series of brisk interviews and writes a book about the place with plenty of references to primitive society and the tribal unconscious. To say anything more is, perhaps, inviting confusion. Yet, though the parallels with initiation ceremonies in Polynesia may be exhausted, personal experience has still something to tell.' See Ray, 'Story into Script', *Sight and Sound*, vol. 26 no. 4, Autumn 1956, p. 70.

13 A throwaway line at the end, where Brub tells Lochner that Dix and Laurel will never forget Mildred Atkinson, has always seemed to me to have the same casual cynicism toward a dead woman who was the motor of the plot as the psychiatrist's dismissal of Marion Crane at the end of *Psycho* as just 'the girl' the swamp got, inert matter thrown aside. For other suggestions of parallels between Ray and Hitchcock, see Michael Wilmington's essay on Ray in *Velvet Light Trap*, no. 11, Winter 1974, pp. 35–40.

14 Stefano Masi, *Nicholas Ray* (Florence: La Nuova Italia, 1983), pp. 30–1.

15 Alain Ménil, 'Le violent', *Cinématographe*, no. 91, July–August 1983, pp. 58–9.

16 Jean Wagner, *Nicholas Ray* (Paris: Rivages, 1987), pp. 97–8.

17 Geoff Andrew, *The Films of Nicholas Ray* (London: Charles Letts & Co., 1991), p. 59.

18 Ibid., p. 56.

19 Quoted in William H. Lyles, *Putting Dell on the Map: A History of the Dell Paperbacks* (Westport, CT: Greenwood Press, 1983).

20 For background on the independents, see Janet Staiger, 'Individualism versus Collectivism', *Screen*, vol. 24 no. 4–5, July–October 1983, pp. 68–79; the contemporary analysis of Fredric Marlowe, 'The Rise of the Independents in Hollywood', *Penguin Film Review*, no. 3, August 1947, pp. 72–5; and the 'Hollywood Independents' special issue of *Velvet Light Trap*, no. 22, 1986.

21 Allen Eyles, *Humphrey Bogart* (London: Sphere, 1990). In a letter to me (5 November 1992), Dorothy B. Hughes also repeated the Lauren Bacall rumour: 'I admit I did envision Betty [Bacall] as the girl. So did Bogart, he told me he wanted her but Warners wouldn't release her. One of those Hollywood feuds of which there were many. But I think Gloria Grahame was superb. A fine actor she'. Nicholas Ray, in his interview with Michael Wilmington (*Velvet Light Trap*, Fall 1973) also recounts a weird story in which Ginger Rogers originally had the role: 'I refused to meet Harry Cohn [head of Columbia, the distribution company for *In a Lonely Place*] because Bogart was president of the company [Santana], and I said, "Look, you're the president of the company. Bobby Lord's the producer. That's enough bosses for me." And they came to me and said, "Hey, Nick, it's getting embarrassing. Harry Cohn wants to meet you." And I said, "Well, all right – if it's getting embarrassing for him." And I went into his office, and I said, "Well, finally I meet a legend." And he said, "Come on in and have a drink. I hear you're having a

problem with the leading lady." I said, "I don't have a problem. I just don't want Ginger Rogers." "Who do you want?" "Gloria Grahame." "You're married to her, huh?" "What the hell does that have to do with it? She's right for the part." He said, "Well, ask your man [Howard] Hughes to call me." I said, "Why don't you call him?"

Somehow or other, I got a call from Howard saying, "Have Harry Cohn meet me at the corner of Santa Monica and Formosa at midnight in the filling station."

Apparently Harry met him, because he called me about two o'clock in the morning and said, "What the Hell are you trying to do to me? You know what I did with that maniac all night? I drove in that dirty Chevrolet of his up and down the alleys of Bennett and Santa Monica. All night long!" I wish I'd been there. Because here were two tycoons, two robber barons – who hadn't talked to each other for five years. And he said, "You tell him the next time we have a meeting, we have it in my home."

The next time they had it in Harry's home. Harry had a bedroom and a living room on the second floor of his mansion, which was about one golf course long and half a golf course wide.

He called me the next day and said, "You know what that crazy son of a bitch did last night?"

And I said, "No. What'd he do, Harry?"

"Well, he saw this window over on the far right side of my room. It was open about a foot. The only one outside was my watchman. He goes over and pushes down the damn window so we won't be heard by anybody!"

"What happened?"

"Well, I made a deal."

And my wife got a job.'

(In her autobiography, Ginger Rogers makes no mention of having been cast in *In a Lonely Place*. In fact, she expresses regret at having missed her one chance to play opposite Bogart in a film from 1940, *It All Came True*. Ray's story – like so many great Hollywood anecdotes – remains totally fascinating and totally unconfirmed.)

22 Antoine de Baecque, *Les Cahiers du cinéma: histoire d'une revue. Tome 1: A l'assaut du cinéma, 1951–1959* (Paris: Cahiers du cinéma, 1991), pp. 187–8.

23 François Truffaut, *The Films in My Life* (New York: Simon and Schuster, 1978), pp. 170–1.

24 Wagner, *Nicholas Ray*, p. 55.

25 Penelope Houston and John Gillett, 'Conversation with Nicholas Ray and Joseph Losey', *Sight and Sound*, vol. 30 no. 4, Autumn 1961, pp. 182–7.

26 Bertrand Tavernier and Jean-Pierre Coursodon, *50 Ans de Cinéma Américain* (Paris: Editions Nathan, 1991), p. 217.

27 Letter of 21 March 1949, quoted in Robert Sklar, *City Boys: Cagney, Bogart, Garfield* (Princeton, NJ: Princeton University Press, 1992), p. 249.

28 Bernard Eisenschitz, *Roman américain: les vies de Nicholas Ray* (Paris: Christian Bourgois, 1990), p. 174.

29 Ray's own notes on Mel state: 'Relationship with him must be warm – endure everything – friend to the death.' Art Smith, who played Mel, was an old friend of Ray's from his radical theatre days in the 1930s. In another interweaving of art and life, Smith would go on from this film about pressure and paranoia in Hollywood to being blacklisted in the 1950s after being named as a Communist by Ray's big buddy, Elia Kazan.

30 Adriano Aprà *et al.*, 'Interview with Nicholas Ray', *Movie*, no. 9, 1963, p. 16.

CREDITS

· ·

In a Lonely Place

USA
1950
Production company
Santana Pictures
A Columbia Pictures
Corporation Presentation
US release
17 May 1950
Distributor (US)
Columbia
UK release
19 June 1950
Distributor (UK)
Columbia
Copyright date
1 August 1950
Producer
Robert Lord
Associate producer
Henry S. Kesler
Director
Nicholas Ray
Assistant director
Earl Bellamy
Screenplay
Andrew Solt from the novel
In a Lonely Place by Dorothy
B. Hughes, published in
1947
Adaptation
Edmund H. North
Script supervisor
Charlsie Bryant
**Photography
(black and white)**
Burnett Guffey
Camera operator
Gert Anderson
Gaffer
William Johnson
Grip
Walter Meins

Music
George Antheil
Musical direction
Morris Stoloff
Orchestration
Ernest Gold
Editor
Viola Lawrence
Art director
Robert Peterson
Gowns
Jean Louis
Make-up
Clay Campbell
Sound
William Kiernan
Sound engineer
Howard Fogetti
Technical adviser
Rodney Amateau
94 minutes
8,375 feet

Humphrey Bogart
Dixon Steele
Gloria Grahame
Laurel Gray
Frank Lovejoy
Brub Nicolai
Carl Benton Reid
Captain Lochner
Art Smith
Mel Lippman
Jeff Donnell
Sylvia Nicolai
Martha Stewart
Mildred Atkinson
Robert Warwick
Charlie Waterman
Morris Ankrum
Lloyd Barnes
William Ching
Ted Barton
Steven Geray
Paul

Hadda Brooks
Singer
Charles Cane
Irate husband in car
Frank Marlowe
Dave, car parker at Paul's
Billy Gray
Young boy
Cosmo Sardo
Greg, bartender
Lewis Howard
Junior
Alice Talton
Frances Randolph
George Davis
Waiter at Paul's
Robert O. Davis
Street waterer
Ruth Warren
Effie, cleaning lady
Jack Reynolds
Henry Kesler
Ruth Gillette
Martha, masseuse
Don Hamin
John Mason, young driver
Myron Healey
Post Office clerk
Robert Lowell
Airline clerk
Pat Barton
2nd hatcheck girl
David Bond
Surgeon Richards
Guy Beach
Swan

Mike Romanoff
Himself
Arno Frey
Joe
Melinda Erickson
Tough girl
Jack Jahries
Officer

With Tony Layng, Laura K. Brooks, Jack Santoro, Evelyn Underwood, Hazel Boyne, Mike Lally, John Mitchum, Joy Hallward, Allen Pinson, Oliver Cross, June Vincent.

Working title:
Behind This Mask

The print of *In a Lonely Place* in the National Film Archive was specially acquired from Columbia Pictures.
(Credits prepared by Markku Salmi.)

BIBLIOGRAPHY

a. On *In a Lonely Place*

Draper, Ellen. '*In a Lonely Place*', *Cinema Texas Program Notes* (21 April 1980), pp. 61–5.

McVay, Doug. 'Outcast State: Nicholas Ray's *In a Lonely Place*', *Bright Lights*, no. 7 (1978), pp. 4–7.

Ménil, Alain. '*Le violent*', *Cinématographe*, no. 91 (July–August 1983), pp. 58–9.

Palmer, James W. '*In a Lonely Place*: Paranoia in the Dream Factory', *Literature/Film Quarterly*, vol. 13 no. 3, 1985, pp. 200–7.

Perkins, V. F. 'In a Lonely Place', in Ian Cameron (ed.), *The Movie Book of Film Noir* (London: Studio Vista, 1992), pp. 222–31.

Telotte, J. P. 'Film noir and the dangers of discourse', *Voices in the Dark: The Narrative Patterns of Film Noir* (Urbana, IL: University of Illinois Press, 1989), pp. 189–94.

Williamson, Judith. 'Lean Cuts', *New Statesman*, 22 January 1988, pp. 27–8.

b. On Nicholas Ray

Allen, Blaine. *Nicholas Ray: A Guide to References and Resources* (Boston: G. K. Hall, 1989).

Andrew, Geoff. *The Films of Nicholas Ray* (London: Charles Letts & Co., 1991).

Bastide, Jean-Pierre. 'Un étranger ici-bas: Nicholas Ray en Amérique', *Études cinématographiques*, no. 8–9, 1961, pp. 17–51.

Coursodon, Jean-Pierre. *American Directors*, vol. 2 (New York: McGraw-Hill, 1983), pp. 306–13.

Eisenschitz, Bernard. *Roman américain: les vies de Nicholas Ray* (Paris: Christian Bourgois, 1990). (English translation forthcoming from Faber & Faber.)

Elsaesser, Thomas. 'Nicholas Ray', *Brighton Film Review*, no. 19, April 1970, pp. 13–16, and no. 20, May 1970, pp. 15–16.

Jousse, Thierry. 'Nicholas Ray: éclats de vie', *Cahiers du cinéma*, no. 430, April 1990, pp. 76–81.

Masi, Stefano. *Nicholas Ray* (Florence: La Nuova Italia, 1983).

Perkins, V. F. 'The Cinema of Nicholas Ray', *Movie*, no. 9, 1963, pp. 5–11.

Rosenbaum, Jonathan.

'Nicholas Ray', in Richard Roud (ed.), *Cinema: a Critical Dictionary* volume 2 (London: Secker & Warburg, 1980), pp. 807–12. (This is a revision of Rosenbaum's influential 'Circle of Pain: the Cinema of Nicholas Ray', *Sight and Sound*, vol 42 no. 4, Autumn 1973, pp. 218–21.)

Serceau, Daniel and Serceau, Michel. *Nicholas Ray: Architecte de l'Espace, Architecte du Temps* (Amiens: Editions Corps Puce, 1989).

Truchaud, François. *Nicholas Ray* (Paris: Editions Universitaires, 1965).

Wagner, Jean. *Nicholas Ray* (Paris: Rivages, 1987).

Wilmington, Michael. 'Nicholas Ray: The Years at RKO', *Velvet Light Trap*, no. 10, Fall 1973, pp. 46–53, and no. 11, Winter 1974, pp. 35–40.

c. Interviews with Ray

Aprà, Adriano *et al.* 'Interview with Nicholas Ray', *Movie*, no. 9 (1963), pp. 14–25.

Bitsch, Charles. 'Entretien avec Nicholas Ray', *Cahiers du cinéma*, no. 89, November 1958, pp. 2–14. (Partial translation in the 'Nicholas Ray' dossier in Jim Hillier (ed.), *Cahiers du cinéma: The Fifties: Neo-Realism, Hollywood, New Wave* (London: Routledge and Kegan Paul/British Film Institute, 1985.)

Goodwin, Michael and Wise, Naomi. 'Nicholas Ray, Rebel!', *Take One*, vol. 5 no. 6, January 1977, pp. 7–16, 18–21.

Houston, Penelope and Gillett, John. 'Conversation with Nicholas Ray and Joseph Losey', *Sight and Sound*, vol. 30 no. 4, Autumn 1961, pp. 182–7. Reprinted in Andrew Sarris (ed.), *Interviews with Film Directors* (New York: Bobbs-Merrill, 1967), pp. 269–79; and in *Hollywood Voices: Interviews with Film Directors* (London: Secker and Warburg, 1971).

Wilmington, Michael. 'Nicholas Ray on the Years at RKO', *Velvet Light Trap*, no. 10, Fall 1973, pp. 54–5.

(A collection of some of Ray's writings, lectures, interviews and classroom commentaries is forthcoming as *I Was Interrupted: Nicholas Ray on Making Movies* from University of California Press.)

**BFI Film Classics '. . . could scarcely be improved upon . . .
informative, intelligent, jargon-free companions.'**
The Observer

Each book in the BFI Film Classics series honours a great film from the history of world cinema – *Singin' in the Rain, Citizen Kane, Brief Encounter, Les enfants du paradis*. With four new titles published each spring and autumn, the series is rapidly building into a collection representing some of the best writing on film.

If you would like to receive further information about future BFI Film Classics or about other books on film, media and popular culture from BFI Publishing, please fill in your name and address and return the card to the BFI*.

No stamp is needed if posted in the UK, Channel Islands, or Isle of Man.

NAME

ADDRESS

POSTCODE

*North America: Please return your card to;
Indiana University Press, Attn: LPB, 601 N Morton Street, Bloomington, IN 47401-3797

PN 1997 .I4733 P65 1993 c.1
Polan, Dana B., 1953-
In a lonely place

DATE DUE

GAYLORD   PRINTED IN U.S.A.